"I wish I had this book when I started in the salon business. It would have saved me a lot of heartaches."—Stylist Kim Pelt, Fort Worth, TX

"Ron Sturgeon taught me more about how to grow a service business in the four years I served with him on a board than I learned in twenty years of managing my business. He's a master strategist." —Carol Roedder, Business Owner, URG Board Member, St. Louis, MO

"Ron's business advice is invaluable, and his ability to make complex things simple, coupled with his intuitive ability to understand customers and employees, putting it all into a marketing and business growth plan make him a brilliant mentor and author." —Bill Stevens, Business Consultant, Burleson, TX

"This book is filled with ideas to build your salon business from a great stylist and a business guru. It made me rethink how I am pricing my services."—Stylist Soven Garlock, Samson Park, TX

"I love how Ron thinks big to do big, and as business people we simply don't have training in how to think like that." —Dixon Thayer, Consultant, Unionville, PA

"Just one of the ideas from the marketing plan yielded three new clients in less than a week!"—Renee Rochin, Sola Salon, an independent salon owner, Highland Village, TX

"They don't teach this stuff in school. It's like getting a degree in salon management!"—Stylist Liz Hamell, Fort Worth, TX

# THE INSIDER'S GUIDE TO EARNING $100K AS A SELF-EMPLOYED SALON PRO

## ONE MUST-DO
## AND FOUR PITFALLS YOU MUST AVOID
## TO BE SUCCESSFUL AND RETIRE WITH A NEST EGG

### INCLUDES
### A STEP-BY-STEP SALON MARKETING PLAN
### TO KEEP YOUR BOOK FULL

## RON STURGEON & DAVID BLACKSTOCK

MISSION POSSIBLE PUBLISHING

FORT WORTH

2018

To all of the salon professionals who want a more satisfying and rewarding career but are unsure of exactly what to do next. I hope my experience rising from homelessness to start and build successful businesses will give you the roadmap you need.

R. S.


To my mentor, Jay Wallace; my godmother, Ruta Lee; my best friend, Gennifer Flowers; and my soulmate, Tony Colbert.

D. B.

Published by

**Mission Possible Publishing**

**P.O. Box 37007**

**Haltom City, Texas 76117**

**For more information, contact Jennifer Knittel at**

**Jenniferk@rdsinvestments.com or**

**817-834-3625, Ext. 232**

Copyright © 2018 Ron Sturgeon
First edition: February 2018

For reseller information including quantity discounts and bulk sales, please contact the publisher.

ISBN: 978-0-9851112-4-3
Manufactured in the United States of America
10 9 8 7 6 5 4 3 2 1
First Edition

# Contents

# ACKNOWLEDGMENTS

**Writers**
Ron Sturgeon, David Blackstock with all others (Jennifer Knittel,
Linda Allen, Veronica Bivens Evans, Leah Euston, Katie Goff,
Christina Lasater and Kim Pelt) by Eric Anderson

**Project Manager**
Ron Sturgeon

**Editors**
Eric Anderson, Paula Cooper & Kelly Conway

**Cover Designs**
Ron Sturgeon & 99 Designs

**Publisher**
Mission Possible Publishing

Special thanks to the dozens of friends and colleagues who voted,
edited, and advised on everything from the cover's design to the
marketing campaign.

# Forewords

When I decided to become an entrepreneur and open a State Farm agency in Fort Worth, I was fortunate to be able to turn to Ron Sturgeon. His friendship, mentoring, and advice have helped me become successful more quickly.

Ron Sturgeon has had an enviable business career. He has started, grown, and sold businesses to Fortune 500 companies. As a consultant, he has helped countless business owners reach greater success. He was featured recently on CNBC's *Blue Collar Millionaires*® program and his marketing advice has appeared in *Inc.* Magazine. He is the author of nine books, most of them for the owners of small businesses.

Ron's father died when he was in high school and left Ron $1,500 and a VW bug. The death of his father left Ron homeless. Ron taught himself to fix the VW and soon started his first business, a VW-repair shop.

When he realized he was making as much selling parts from his boneyard of VWs as he was from fixing cars, Ron turned his garage into an auto-salvage yard. He grew that business from one employee into one of the largest yards in the United States, before selling it to Ford.

Ron's life is a testament to a fact that every entrepreneur should take to heart: No matter where you start, you can become a great business success. A lack of education will not stop you if you have a strong enough desire and work ethic. This book was written to help salon professionals like you become as successful as possible.

Ron is one of America's best business strategists. He has a way of boiling down complex business issues to their essence and his advice has always been spot on. Whether you are a newly licensed beauty professional or someone with decades in the profession, you can improve your business by reading and following the advice in this book. In its pages you will learn the greatest mistake that any beauty professional can make. You will discover the traps that hold many professionals back from achieving lasting success. This book also includes a dozen of Ron's best articles from his syndicated column about business.

One of the pain points many independent stylists have is how to market. The final chapter of this book includes Ron's step-by-step plan to bring you new clients. In addition, you will also hear advice from several independent beauty professionals who are building successful salon businesses. Fort Worth's premier celebrity stylist, David Blackstock, drawing from his three decades behind the chair, also shares seven tips that will speed you on the path to success. I have also contributed an article about goal setting for business owners.

I applaud you for picking this book up. It shows you have the desire to make your beauty business all that it can be. I wish you great success. Apply the principles in this book and watch your beauty business grow!

Linda Allen
Linda Allen State Farm Agency
Fort Worth, Texas
Author of *Out with Customer Service; In with People Service*

When Ron asked me to write a foreword for this book, I was eager to do it. I've known and worked with Ron for decades and can say he is one of the most thoughtful and committed people with regard to helping other business owners become more successful.

Ron brings a rare balance of hands-on experience across a wide range of industries. This gives him advantaged insight into how to help other entrepreneurs regardless of the business they're in.

A truly unique individual, Ron has consistently exceeded expectations. I recommend anyone who wishes to achieve breakthrough success follow his business advice.

Dixon Thayer
Venture Capitalist
Co-Founder, Medovation Capital Resources
Unionville, Pennsylvania

David Blackstock has been my stylist, and my friend, for more than two decades. His talent is exceeded only by his innate ability to know each of his client's needs. This ability has directly contributed to his enduring success as a personal stylist to celebrities.

David offers the expertise of a true professional, combined with the loyalty and kindness of a best friend. This mix of gift and familiarity makes David an artist who seamlessly brings out the best in each of his clients.

David's entrepreneurial success should inspire other stylists to shoot for the stars and to follow his lead.

Ruta Lee
Actress, Dancer, and Philanthropist
Fort Worth, Texas

# INTRODUCTION

Ruta Lee and David
(Photo Credit: Alan Mercer)

I have been a stylist for more than thirty years. I was lucky to be mentored into the business and to have the opportunity to learn from Mr. Jay Wallace, an outstanding Fort Worth-based stylist known for both his candor and his kindness.

Early on, I decided that I wanted to become a celebrity stylist and worked toward that goal by volunteering to work at a Fort Worth theatre, *Casa Manana*. I worked hard to make my clients shine and was rewarded with their trust. Gradually, my friends like Ruta Lee began to recommend me to their friends and I was on my way to building a following among the clientele I most wanted to serve.

Over the years, I have had the honor to work with some wonderful people: Gennifer Flowers, Debbie Reynolds, Joan Rivers, Ruth Buzzi, and many others.

A celebrity stylist plays many roles -- friend, advisor, confidante, even bodyguard. Of course, it also requires helping your client be ready to look her or his best. I regularly travel to New Orleans and to Los Angeles to take care of my clients.

Gennifer Flowers and David Blackstock
(Photo Credit: Alan Mercer)

When I first started in the industry, I had a desire to own my own salon, and I achieved that goal. At one point in my career, I bought the salon where I worked from a friend of mine. My friend stayed on as I made updates to the salon. This was difficult because he was deeply invested in the salon he had created. That experience taught me a lot about being a salon owner, even though it cost me a friendship.

If your ambition is to become a successful beauty professional and to own your own salon, I applaud you. You will find lots of helpful advice in the pages of this book. However, I would also caution you to think about what you really enjoy about the business. You may find, as I have, that your real satisfaction is working with your clients. Managing a staff added a lot of complexity to what I wanted to be simple. My answer has been to lease a salon suite and focus on serving the clients in my chair.

That you are reading this book means you have ambition to become more successful. I am eager to share some of the lessons I have learned from over thirty years as a celebrity stylist. I hope the advice in these pages will help you build your following and become as successful as you wish to be.

David Blackstock
Celebrity Stylist
Blackstock Studios @ Phenix Salon
Fort Worth, Texas

# Chapter 1

# One Must-Do for Salon Professionals

*"In every success story, you will find someone who has made a courageous decision."*

—Peter F. Drucker, Management Guru

If you were to think about all of your experiences as a salon professional or as a customer, you could probably come up with a big list of career-enhancing behaviors for salon professionals:

- Salon pros who seek to become well known as the best at particular services...

- Salon pros who market themselves online and share testimonials and pictures of their work on social media...

- Salon pros who are habitually early and eager to get to the salon...

- Salon pros who dress professionally and project the right image...

- Salon pros who think about the lifetime value of each client…

- Salon pros who pre-book the next appointment before their clients leave the salon….

- Salon pros who devote themselves to continuing education and to stay current…

These are all things that salon pros should do. They will all make you more successful. However, they are not the most important thing that a salon owner must do to reach the elite level of earnings.

The thing all salon professionals must do is illustrated by this story told by legendary sales trainer Zig Ziglar. Zig said, if you put fleas in a glass jar and close the lid, they will try to escape. For hours, those fleas will jump with all their might, hit the lid, and drop back into the jar.

After a day or two, however, even the dumbest fleas wises up. It learns to jump just high enough to avoid the lid. At that point, Zig used to say, the lid could come off. The fleas would never jump high enough to escape because of what they believed.

Whether you have just earned your state license or have been a salon professional for many years, you must avoid selecting a business model that **limits your possibilities**, **puts a lid on your earnings**, and **robs you of your right to direct your salon career**.

If you have strong technical skills, a good work ethic, and solid people skills, salon owners will eagerly offer you a job as an hourly employee or as an hourly-plus-commission employee. If you have ambition, work ethic, and professional-level skills, the biggest mistake you can make is to say *"yes."*

A *yes* gets you a salon job, and not a high-paying one, instead of a salon career and certainly not your own business. Consider how long you have trained to learn your craft. You have invested a lot of time and money to get the skills to be a beauty professional.

Make sure you earn what those skills are worth. The fastest-growing segment of the salon business is salon-suite rental because many beauty professionals have discovered that the path to real earnings starts with building a beauty business that is really their own.

Salon pros chose the suite-rental model because independents don't have a cap on their earnings. They don't split earnings with the salon's owner. They are free to choose which product lines to carry and free to keep all of the money their product sales generate. When a salon employee moves on, the salon owner assigns those clients to another employee. An independent is building a client base that belongs to him or her. Imagine how many clients you can accumulate in 10 or 15 years of working steadily at it?

Why give those clients to a salon owner? They are yours! Even if it takes some time to build up your following, eventually you will get there. When you do, you will have a viable, professional, successful business of your own with assets that are yours. And let's not forget that you want to be able to eventually **own your own business and your real estate** so that you can rent to others, as you pile up the equity and cash for a wonderful retirement.

In these pages, you will meet several top independent salon professionals. David Blackstock is one of America's most sought-after celebrity stylists. You will learn his secrets to becoming a top-earning beauty professional. In this book, you will also get the insights of one of Fort Worth's best marketing minds, Ron Sturgeon, a serial entrepreneur and business consultant who recently appeared on CNBC's hit show *Blue Collar Millionaires®*.

In addition, you will hear the advice of five other professionals who are currently building successful followings as independent salon professionals, as well as hearing from a leasing agent, who will share the questions to ask before you sign any lease for a salon space, suite, or chair. Let's get started.

# CHAPTER 2

# FOUR PITFALLS
# YOU MUST AVOID

*"I thank God for my failures. Maybe not at the time, but after some reflection. I never feel like a failure just because something I tried failed."*

—Dolly Parton

As you think about becoming an independent salon professional, I am going to ask you to consider *why* some salon professionals who try to make the jump from employee to independent professional fail.

Before you continue, write three or four reasons you think account for most of these failures and then we can compare lists and think about the ways for you to avoid the four most serious pitfalls that prevent salon professionals for reaching success:

1.

2.

3.

4.

First, some independent beauty professionals fail because they are not as talented as they believe. They are unable to achieve consistently good results for their clients, so they struggle to get clients to book the next appointment and to earn referrals.

Their less-than-wowed customers might not always complain, but they don't come back. When a client tries to give them feedback, they take it personally because they have a distorted view of their skills. The salon workers in this group belong in some other line of work, but they just have not realized it yet.

Readers of this book will likely not fit in that category. Many who become independent professionals have had years of solid salon experience and excelled in beauty school and are very good at serving clients in a salon or spa because they have a passion for the beauty industry. Reading books about success is an indicator that you have the right passion and openness to learning to make a beauty business work. Your skill level likely reflects that passion.

If you are hungry to become better and love the beauty industry, you will likely become a skilled professional, if you are not already in that category. As David Blackstock says, "If you are not blessed with a natural gift for styling hair, you can learn it, and still have an enviable career." That's equally true of other kinds of salon professionals.

✂ ✂ ✂

Sometimes the path to success is different from the one you anticipate. Smart business people are tuned in to what the world tells them about their place in the industry. For example, Allison Bridges, author of *Trade Secrets of the Successful Stylist*, an insightful guide, recognized that she had more aptitude for business management than for styling when learning the first few cuts during her Vidal Sassoon training took her longer than it took some of her peers.

She knew she would have to work extra hard to succeed as a stylist. She was disciplined and became a good stylist, but she was also tuned in enough to make the move into salon management and to get the experience that readied her to become a superstar salon owner.

The second reason independent beauty professionals fail is that they do not do enough pre-launch planning. They may be in a hurry because they are in a bad employment situation and see salon-suite rental as a way to put themselves back in control. It can be, but not for those unwilling to do the hard work of putting pencil to paper and making a business plan based on realistic assumptions.

To avoid this pitfall, you should write a business plan. Meet some salon professionals who rent space where you are considering renting a station or suite. Talk with others who have gone from salon employee to independent. If appropriate, look at the business plans they wrote to refine yours.

If you are not strong in business plan writing, get some help from a mentor. I have started, built, and sold many different kinds of businesses over my more than thirty-year business career. I have never entered any new business without doing a significant amount of planning and that always included writing a business plan. For the same reason that you hire an architect before building a home, you should have a good business plan before you become an independent beauty professional.

The third reason some salon employees don't succeed is that they lack discipline. Instead of keeping the hours promised on their salon's Facebook page, they come and go as they please. If they had a plan for their business, they lack the discipline to do the daily work needed to make that plan happen. Salon customers who find a salon closed when it should be open are apt to move to a more reliable salon professional.

A lack of discipline is a tough pitfall to overcome. A person who does not show up on time every business day is going to struggle as his or her own boss. Discipline can be learned like any other habit, but I would be sure I had that habit before taking the plunge into business ownership.

The final pitfall to avoid, a lack of good marketing, is what kills the most independent service businesses. I think most salon professionals like the artistic side of their work much more than they like doing the work to market services to potential clients. If you are in this group, you can still be successful.

The first part of overcoming this last pitfall is to admit that it applies to you. This book contains some marketing help. I have been highly successful in marketing services and have helped to create a marketing plan that any independent salon professional can adapt and use to generate leads and new clients. That plan is in the final chapter of this book.

If I were a stylist about to go independent, I would be eager to learn all that I could from salon professionals who had built a following. Not every technique that works for another beauty professional will work for you. Be willing to experiment and to measure results by tracking cost-per-lead and cost-per-new-client-acquisition. Both concepts are covered in the chapter of this book that has my Tools for Success articles.

If marketing is not a strength for you, be sure to use some of your time at trade shows for the industry to learn about new ways to build your following. These sessions may be less fun, but they are vitally important to putting money in the bank. Chapter 12 of this book includes a marketing plan and checklists that you can adapt to your business.

One of the most important business lessons I learned early in my career was to surround myself with people who were smarter than I am and who were willing to do those things that I couldn't, wouldn't, or shouldn't. This lesson applies to marketing. If you don't have the writing or graphic-design skills to do quality posts on social media, get help. Don't be afraid to get help with any marketing tasks that you do not do well.

If you are short on cash, you may be able to make a trade of services to get the marketing help you need. Remember that all of your marketing materials — flyers, social media posts, website, Facebook page, StyleSeat, etc. — are a reflection of your business. Make sure they are professional and polished because potential customers will make judgements about your business based on your marketing materials.

Knowing the road ahead makes the journey easier. Think about these pitfalls and the ones on your list. Be proactive in adding to your skills (especially in marketing) so that you reach your goal of earning more and enjoying your work more as an independent salon professional.

## Chapter 3

# Tips from Stylist-to-the-Stars David Blackstock

*"I think the most important thing a woman can have—next to talent, of course—is her hairdresser."*

—Joan Crawford, Actress

Stylist David Blackstock
(Photo credit: Alan Mercer)

When my friend Ron Sturgeon came to me with the idea of writing a book to help stylists be more successful, I was eager to share what I have learned in a long career in the industry. One thing that Ron and I have in common is that we both had early life experiences that caused us to come to adulthood with extraordinary drive to succeed in our chosen professions.

Ron lost a parent when he was in high school and was even homeless during his last year of high school. He learned early the habit of self-reliance and resilience. My early life was tumultuous enough that its bleakness created a strong contrast with the glamour of the stars of movies and television programs that I used as an escape.

Growing up, I struggled to find success in school because I am dyslexic. When the owner of a salon let me come and help after school, I knew that I had found what I wanted to do with my life. It was quite a revelation for a young boy, and a turning point in my life's journey, even if I wasn't cognizant of it at the time.

I have always been single-minded in pursuit of my dream to become a hairdresser because I loved what I was doing, but I also was fearful that I did not have many other career options. I did not see myself working behind a desk and pushing paper, nor did I have the misconception that I would be President of the United States one day. Realism has always been both a burden and gift for me. Therefore, the realization that I longed to not only be a hairdresser, but to truly be one of the best, was most likely what saved me from an otherwise less-than-stellar lifestyle.

I apprenticed my way into the beauty business. I did anything to work in the salon. I swept floors. I washed hair. I washed towels. I ran errands and kept all of the plates spinning so that the professional stylists with whom I worked could do their jobs effectively. My advice to people who are in junior high or high school and think they want a career in the beauty business is to go and volunteer at a salon. A cosmetology education is expensive, and building your business from the ground up takes time and effort. The best way to find out if this path is right for you is to go and get some experience.

My journey in the salon business has been a little different from many of my peers. I apprenticed my way into the profession, worked in a salon, purchased the salon, and eventually decided that the headaches of owning a salon were not worth it. Our industry is changing, and the most successful stylists are not working in a traditional salon environment. I now lease a salon suite and make more income than I did when I had a dozen stylists working for me.

At the end of the day, the expense of owning and operating a salon with actual employed commission stylists just isn't practical any longer; neither for the owner, nor the stylists. Lease your own space, even if you share the expense with another stylist. Keep your expenses low, and keep everything you earn beyond expenses for yourself.

For those already in the business, I would like to share some advice that has helped me achieve an extraordinary level of success. First, I would say that stylists should embrace who they are and be authentic. I'm outspoken, opinionated, and more than a little irreverent. Not everyone gets me, but that's okay. The time I spend with my clients is an experience that many of them enjoy and remember because they know that I will tell it like I see it. I am unique, and so is the client experience that I deliver. It takes too much effort to try to be someone other than myself, and I am confident that my clients know authenticity. In fact, it is a trademark of mine, and I do not believe I would have achieved the success I have today without it.

Second, beauty pros should strive to create a consistent identity. As a colorist, I am known not only for working with a particular line, but for a particular shade. I have a specific identity because I have cultivated that identity. If you try to follow every fad, you won't develop a set of distinct things you are known for (and can charge more for) because people see you as the best in those areas. Be consistent in the identity you project. If your identity is your own, and I highly recommend that it should be, then you never have to be concerned about remembering how to deliver on your brand, which is, at the end of the day, you.

Third, I would advise stylists and other beauty professionals to choose who you associate with carefully. I cannot reiterate this enough. I have always strived to surround myself with people who have good judgement. In salons, you will have plenty of opportunity to associate yourself with people whose lives are filled with drama, so much drama that they don't focus on their clients and their business. In contrast, you have equal opportunity to learn from those who are achieving what you are striving for.

Wherever you work, be friends with the pros who are serious about becoming the best at what they do. Regardless of the level of success you achieve, you can always learn something new from another high-performing professional. Never be too proud to watch, listen, and grow your own talent even more.

Fourth, I would say set and write down your goals. When you want something and focus your energy on it, you will often find that the world opens a path to your goal. Early on, I set a goal of becoming a celebrity stylist. To get there, I volunteered at a local theatre while I was working another gig full-time. At the theatre, I styled the wigs worn by celebrities who appeared in all the shows. Some of my current clients first met me there. Writing out your goals will help you stay focused on them and help you to see the path the world will open for you. If you do not know your destination, it is difficult to chart a course to get there.

Fifth, I would advise stylists to have the courage to dream about what they really want. One of my childhood idols was Joan Rivers. I have always loved her. I decided as a young boy that I wanted to meet her and style her hair. Years later, my childhood dream come true on multiple occasions. I was able to accomplish this goal because I was known for being authentic, loyal, and for having integrity in all that I did. Don't be afraid to dream about what you really want or to share your dreams with people who care about you. When you least expect it, you may very well find your own dreams realized as a result.

Sixth, don't be afraid to promote yourself. When you make a milestone in your career, don't be afraid to share it. After I styled Joan's hair, I shared my pictures with her because it was an amazing experience. How many stylists ever get that chance? Let me add that you are unlikely to be successful just because you are talented, at least in the beginning. No one else cares about whether you make it or not, so you better learn to be willing to talk about yourself and how good you are, and you had better have a plan for marketing yourself. Remember, you are your own brand. It's a noisy marketplace out there; you will have to work HARD to be noticed and build a good following, enough of a following that on any given day you have very few open appointments.

Many stylists whine about there not being enough walk-ins. If you think you are going to have a successful career based only on walk-ins in this business, you are doomed. Walk-ins are just that; people who do not have a current loyalty to any stylist, who wander from salon to salon. Your job, your mission, is to convert that walk-in to your loyal client. I did this by placing myself in the direct path of walk-ins. I worked in a mall salon for the sole purpose of converting as many walk-in as possible into loyal, long-term clients. As soon as I had enough clients to move into a more professional and more lucrative working environment, I did just that. These twenty-five plus years later, I still have clients who I first met when I worked in the mall. Imagine the income they have generated for me during these twenty-five years!

This is not the only technique that I have used. I have also introduced myself to the person in front of me in the checkout line at Target and told them how much I loved their hair and offered them tips to enhance their style, while at the same time mentioning that I am a stylist and handing them a business card. When you're in a commission-based income career, you're in sales. Think of this as "cold calling,"

except you are doing it in person. Not every person will respond by calling you for an appointment. But what if two out of ten do? What if one of those two becomes a lifelong, loyal client who generates an income stream for you for the next 20 years?

This isn't farfetched. I've lived this experience. Do what you have to do to get the client in your chair, and then sell yourself through your talent, your branding, and, of course, your unique authenticity.

Finally, beauty professionals who start to become successful are going to be envied. As you build a great business, you should expect that some other stylists will talk about you in unkind ways. Don't take it personally. Don't let it bother you. Be gracious, stay positive, and keep building your business. You may lose what you thought were friendships. You may become the target of the underachievers and stylists who are not willing to make the sacrifices that you have made to achieve your goals. This is nothing but noise, and you can and should turn it off. Your goal is your own, and no one, absolutely, positively no one, can take it away from you or stop you from achieving it. I did it. I know that you can, too.

I wish you great success and hope these tips will help you identify what is important to you professionally, while inspiring you to take the necessary risks to obtain that which you have set your sights on. Go forth with confidence that for you, the goal-setter, the style-maker, the determined self-starter, anything is possible. Absolutely anything.

## Chapter 4

# The Suite Deal:
# Leasing Space

*"A move toward chair rental is the biggest trend in the salon business today."*

—*American Salon*, November 19, 2015

Jennifer Knittel, Salon-Suite
Leasing Manager

I am the leasing manager for a chain of suite-rental salons. I handle leasing for nine salons that are part of this fast-growing chain.

I regularly present information about salon-suite leasing to beauty school students and salon pros that inquire about leasing space in our salons. I believe strongly that the salon-suite model is right for many licensees who are motivated to build a business. However, it isn't the right path for everyone.

This chapter will take a balanced look at the arguments presented by salons to keep employees from leaving to rent salon stations and suites and address the most important features that those seeking to lease a station or suite should look for when shopping for salon space.

Those urging beauty school graduates to become employees (or to stay employees) in salons certainly have valid arguments on their side. This path is right for the person who needs direction and structure and does not want the responsibilities or the rewards that come with business ownership. It is right for the person content with the amount of money they can earn as an employee in a salon. It offers safety and consistency, and that makes it right for some people.

However, many of the arguments made to keep salon professionals from making the jump to salon suites are fear-based. They include long lists of duties designed to make renting a salon station, and becoming independent, seem impossibly difficult.

To show you what I mean, I would like to share some pictures of slides that come from a typical presentation. I have removed the name of the presenter because my purpose is not to single anyone out, but to address the issues included in typical salon presentations to recruit employees or prevent employees from leaving to rent salon stations or suites.

Many of the presentations feature long lists of duties of independent contractors designed to make employees feel that running their own business is too scary, but a close look at the lists shows many of these duties are not much different from what the professional already does and others are definitely manageable.

Here is the first slide from an association for a salon trade group:

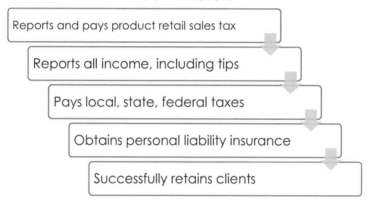

## A Successful Licensed Independent Contractor:

Reports and pays product retail sales tax

Reports all income, including tips

Pays local, state, federal taxes

Obtains personal liability insurance

Successfully retains clients

Everyone should report and pay taxes on retail sales. Some contractors choose to not sell products to avoid this responsibility. Some who do sell product but don't feel confident in this aspect of their business get help from a bookkeeper or use a point of sale system and run a report to make the needed filings.

Everyone should report all income, including tips. This obligation to report income is no different from the one employees have when they do their own personal income taxes and should not prevent you from being a self-employed salon professional.

Salon professionals should also pay the local, state, and federal taxes they owe. Many beauty pros operate as sole proprietors and treat their income as personal income and so they are doing the same tax returns they have always done. Don't let the need to do a tax return be the reason you do not start your own salon business. If paperwork isn't something you enjoy, choose instead to hire a professional to do this for you so you can focus on your customers and building your business.

Personal liability insurance is insurance that pays claims for accidents that cause injury or damage to property. A beauty professional should investigate the cost of the coverage and decide whether it makes sense to carry it. Of the 120 stylists that lease from us at the time of this writing, only a handful have it. Not one has had a claim in the three years that I have been leasing manager. A business owner may want to consider liability insurance, but it is not so difficult to understand or buy that it should stop a salon employee from starting a business if she or he has the ambition to do so.

As far as successfully retaining clients, all salon professionals have to do that. The difference is that the clients belong to you, not your employer, when you are an independent professional.

Let's look at a second slide from the same presenter:

**A Successful Licensed Independent Contractor:**

Maintains appropriate healthcare insurance coverage

Manages client scheduling and payment processing

Develops and manages self-marketing

Purchases and maintains adequate products, materials, and tools

Seeks out continuing education

It is true that a person working in a salon providing health insurance should consider the cost to buy coverage or to get coverage through a spouse. This is a fair point.

Managing client scheduling and payment processing may seem like a big one, but for many of our operators it is as simple as keeping an appointment book and running credit cards through Square or another processor. Both are part of running a business, but neither is rocket science.

Even as employees, salon professionals don't last long unless they have some skill at building a following. Marketing is even more essential for independent salon professionals. At our salons, we provide every operator with a marketing plan because consistent, high-quality marketing is what separates average independent salon professionals from top-earners.

While equipping and maintaining a workspace is important to the independent professional, in many cases, it is not much different from what employees do. Most beauty professionals are skilled at keeping their stations in order and maintaining their tools because it is hard to work efficiently unless you do so.

Sometimes starting up requires investing in some supplies and equipment. Many salon-suite-rental companies offer low-interest or no-interest loans for this option, because it meets the needs of some tenants.

Seeking out continuing education is an obligation for all professionals. Many salons offer useful training and mentoring opportunities. When you go independent, you will be taking on a larger role in your program for self-development. As an independent, you will budget money for your continuing education, but you will also have the freedom to choose which trainings and trade shows to attend without having to get permission from your boss.

I believe passionately in salon suite rental because I have seen the successes of some of those who have leased space in our salons. It is true that becoming a business owner is not as simple as working for someone else. It does take more work, but it also offers greater rewards. After all, nothing truly worthwhile is easy. Building a salon business as an independent isn't easy, but it is not as hard as some presentations make it seem.

In addition, many of the presentations given by representatives of salon schools affiliated with salon chains do not always tell the full story about what salon professionals can earn as independents versus what they are earning as salon employees.

This slide is typical of the comparisons:

**Breaking Down the Numbers**
TYPICAL EXAMPLE OF SUITE RENTAL "BREAK EVEN CALCULATOR"
Includes Additional Real World Factors

| Service Data Assumptions: | INDEPENDENT CONTRACTOR/SUITE RENTAL SCENARIO | EMPLOYEE SCENARIO |
|---|---|---|
| Avg. No. of Monthly Clients (Assumes 60% of employee scenario) | 75 | 125 |
| Average Service Price | $65 | $65 |
| ESTIMATED FINANCIAL SCENERAIO CALCULATIONS | | |
| Revenue/Compensation: | | |
| Total Service Revenue | $4,875 | $8,125 |
| Less Salon Service Charge | N/A | ($813) |
| Total Service Revenue After Service Charge | $4,875 | ($7,313) |
| Employee Commission Earned at 43% | N/A | $3,144 |
| Retail Sales Revenue (3 per day, 20 days, $10 each) | $600 | |
| Retail Sales Commission (10%, 3 per day, 20 days, $10 each) | | $60 |
| Tip Income on Service Revenue at 15% average | $731 | |
| Total Revenue/Compensation Before other deductions | $6,206 | $4,423 |
| Expenses/Withholdings | | |
| Average Federal, State, Local Income Tax and FICA Taxes | ($2,288) | ($1,025) |
| Healthcare/Affordable Care Act Provision | ($150) | ($150) |
| Average Suite Rental | ($1,400) | N/A |
| Product Costs/Supplies (10% of Total Service Revenue) | ($488) | |
| Total Estimated Monthly Net Income/Compensation | $1,881 | $3,248 |

Source: PBA Advocacy Renter Education Guide 2014

Here's what those looking at the slide should notice first. The independent contractor serves only 60% of the customers that the employee does. I would contend that, while it does take time to build a following as an independent, independents do not lose any capacity for work when they become independent. They still have just as many appointments in the book. Many of the independents that rent salon spaces at the salons where I am leasing manager actually serve more clients than they did as employees because they are motivated by the fact that they are not giving an owner 57% of the revenue they generate and paying an $813 salon fee to the owner.

The retail revenue line shows that employees are earning $60 for selling $600 dollars of product with margins that should be at 50% or more. Many of those who lease space do well selling product because they consistently demonstrate it and offer it to their clients. They also like being able to choose the lines they want to carry.

This break-even analysis also likely overstates the amount of tax a contractor will pay. While it is true that an independent will pay FICA taxes on his or her 1040, the independent can also deduct business expenses so that taxes are only paid on net earnings. This example also includes local income taxes. Some cities have them, but most parts of the United States have only federal and state taxes on income.

For insurance, the breakdown shows that both the employee and the independent contractor are paying the penalty for not having insurance under the Affordable Care Act. Some stylists choose not to have health insurance; some get it through spouses, so whether this fee applies depends on individual circumstances.

The suite rental cost suggested by this break-even analysis is significantly higher than the average monthly rent at our salons or the dozen or so competitive suite rental salons that I monitor. Our weekly average rent is $165, which equates to $714.45 per month because there are 4.3 weeks in a month. The $1,400 number this analysis uses is almost twice what is typical from my experience.

The lesson that I draw from this is that anyone considering becoming an independent should do their own break-even analysis with realistic projections and real numbers. The analysis that shows you how much less you are going to make may assume you are going to serve 60% fewer customers and unrealistically inflate rent and other expenses. Run your own numbers. Talk to other independent professionals who can give you a realistic picture of what the numbers should be.

You should ask yourself these questions before you make the jump:

## Should You Become an Independent Contractor?

| | | |
|---|---|---|
| What are my realistic income projections? | What are the associated costs? | How many clients would I need to make a profit? |

| | |
|---|---|
| How much work is involved? | What are the risks and benefits? |

The truth is that owning a business is hard work. It takes some grit to be successful, but the numbers are very good for independents who are willing to work. For example, at our salons, weekly rents for a station start at less than the average cost of one cut and color. A stylist who can book one cut and color has paid their weekly rent!

Let's get real. A stylist who cannot book a few such appointments per week is in the wrong profession. However, one who is willing to do the work to build a following, can make an excellent living and can enjoy the freedom and financial security that comes with owning a successful business.

I always tell those considering the risk, if you can do one color and one cut per week, you can likely pay your rent, and everything else you take in that week is yours!

If you do decide to go independent, drawing on my experience as a leasing agent, I would like to share with you some of the attributes you should look for if you choose to lease a salon suite or station and some of the things to ask about in the lease:

- **Desirable location** – Is the salon highly visible in a high-traffic area? Will it be convenient for you and for your clients? Is it in an area with a large enough population nearby to attract strong walk-in traffic? The location matters but it is not as critical as some believe. If you are doing the right marketing and serving your clients properly, you will have a following willing to come to see you wherever you set up shop. You will not be relying on walk-ins but the many customers who ask for you because your book is full. However, it is important that the location be easy to find.

- **Leasing options** - For example, some operators want to start their business part-time and lease a station for a few days, a week, or one week a month. Does the salon have these options? For longer leases, what are the options and what move-in specials are offered?

- **24-7 Access** – Most salon pros will get that last minute call from someone who needs an emergency service. Can you get in to your space to work on weekends or at night? All of our salons offer 24-7 access.

- **Marketing Help** – How much help does the salon offer you in the area of attracting new clients? Do they offer professionals a web page or ways to promote on the salon web page? Are they working to make sure the salon can be found by online searches?

- **Amenities** – Are the salon spaces up to date? Does the property project the kind of image that you want for your business? Do the suites have complimentary WIFI and televisions to make your clients comfortable while you are working on them?

- **Termination Clause** – What if you need to terminate the lease early? What are your obligations? Be sure you read the lease carefully and ask any questions you have. A lease that has a specific penalty (like a specific number of months or weeks of rent) is better than one that leaves you on the hook for all of the remaining months if you have to terminate a long lease near the start. Be sure to understand the termination clause and any notice requirements before you sign a lease for salon space.

- **Special Situations** - What if you get pregnant and cannot work? Does the salon suite have a maternity leave program in the lease? How does it work if you miss time working because of a pregnancy?

When you are shopping for lease space, talk with the professionals in the salons you are considering. Read the lease carefully and ask any questions you have. I wish you great success in finding the right space to build your beauty business!

# CHAPTER 5

# STYLIST AND MAKE-UP ARTIST
# VERONICA BIVENS EVANS

*"Successful stylists look successful."*

—Veronica Bivens Evans, Divine Beauty

Veronica Bivens Evans, Owner
Divine Beauty

My name is Veronica Bivens Evans. I have been in the beauty business for 30 years and have been doing hair and makeup at Divine Beauty, my salon on South Cooper Street in Arlington, Texas, since 2009. I had some advantages starting a beauty business because I come from a family of successful entrepreneurs and was able to learn some business skills while I was growing up. However, regardless of your background, you can be successful in leasing space if you work hard and take care of your business.

My advice to those seeking success in the beauty business is to begin with yourself. If you want to be successful, you have to project an image of success. Successful stylists look successful. They don't leave the house unless they are dressed and made up. The small details matter. If you don't look right, why would anyone hire you as a stylist? If your makeup isn't done right, why would anyone trust you to do theirs?

Take time to make sure that you are completely put together every day. Don't think that you can skip a day because you're not working at the salon. We all know that is the day you will run into your client at Target, and they will notice how you look. Dress to impress every day. Have the look that your clients aspire to have.

Another area that anyone with ambition to build a following should focus on is what kind of experience his or her client has in the salon. The tagline of my business is "Come Experience Your Divine Appointment." With that promise in mind, I do all that I can to make sure that my business is as inviting a place as possible.

I'm in early. My station is neat. I am there to greet my client with a smile and to make sure that she or he enjoys coming to see me. Even if I have a lot on my mind, I stay positive and stay focused on making that experience as good as it can be for the person in my chair.

In my time in the salon business, I have seen some people rent suites and become very successful, and I have seen others who never get out of the starting gate. The biggest difference is that those who make it are hungry. They don't turn away a walk in because it is 5:00 P.M. and they want to go home. They don't say no to a client who has a last-minute date and wants to be beautiful.

I don't ever turn anyone away. The reason is simple. I have had some of my clients for 30 years. Consider how much I have earned from that client who comes to me every two months for 30 years. When I think about clients, I think about the business that I will do with them over a lifetime. If you think of the last-minute appointment that way, you make time. It's true, not all of those who land in your chair become regulars, but if you are doing your business right, a large number should.

Another thing that separates successful professionals from the rest is that they get the add-on sale. Selling salon-quality professional products is an important part of my business. I manage inventories so that I have what I need, and I demonstrate product that I recommend to everyone who sits in my chair. If you are a stylist not selling product, you are not earning what you should be earning. The right products will help your clients maintain their look and they will be grateful to you for the recommendation. Be consistent and ask for the product sale.

Finally, I would advise anyone thinking of becoming an independent beauty professional to commit to continuing education. You can't win in a competitive marketplace if you don't know the trends because you didn't have time to go to a trade show. I love going to continuing education classes because I know I am going to learn something and meet other professionals who are serious about getting better at what they do. Make time for it.

# Chapter 6

# Leah Euston, Fit and Fancy Med Spa

*"Your clients buy you before they buy any services."*

—Leah Euston

Leah Euston, Fit and Fancy Med Spa

I am Leah Euston. I am the owner of Fit & Fancy Med Spa at Salon & Spa Galleria in Grapevine, Texas. I am 26 years old and started in the beauty business when I was 16. I was enrolled in a vocational program in high school and found that I was most drawn to the parts of the curriculum that dealt with skin care.

After high school, I joined the military and was deployed as a logistics specialist. This experience taught me a lot about managing people and processes, both of which have helped me to be a better businessperson. I initially created a mobile spa business in Atlanta before deciding to lease space and open a med spa.

The decision to be in business for myself was an easy one for me. I am the child of immigrants from Jamaica. Even though I was born in the United States, I have ample experience with how hard it is for people working for others in Jamaica to earn enough to get above subsistence level. Leasing space and having my own med spa lets me "create my own lane" and have a path to an income level that will give me financial security and lets me build a business that will be my legacy.

One of the critical pieces of advice I would give to other beauty professionals who are thinking of making the jump from employee to independent-owner is to be aggressive in getting any education that you need to be successful building a business. Even though I had significant experience in the industry, I found an online program and earned a degree in health and beauty management because I wanted formal training that would help me make my med spa a success. If you lack a needed skill, get the training or hire someone to help you in the areas you are deficient.

Having a successful med spa means that I have to evaluate and hire employees. I believe strongly that owners should hold certifications in all the services done at their spas. Right now, I have three licenses and 12 certifications, and I am in the process of earning three more licenses. I need to hold these certifications and licenses so that I can evaluate applicants and make sure they are performing services up to standard. Having them also means I can jump in and do a service if an employee is out or needs assistance.

Another piece of advice I would give to all beauty professionals is to recognize that your clients are buying you before they buy any services from you. Recognize that you are a brand. When I opened my med spa, I hired a consultant to review my site plan. The consultant said that I was devoting too much space to my consultation area.

I devote a lot of attention to making sure that my consultation area *wows* clients. I am careful that it reflects my brand even in the smallest details. I decided to ignore that advice from the consultant because the consultation is the most critical part of what I do at the salon.

It creates confidence in the client that they are in the right place. During the consult, I close the sale on me, a sale that precedes the sale of any services. Whatever your specialty, become excellent at consultation and consider laying out your space in a way that helps you make your prospective client confident in you.

I would also tell beauty professionals that they better be able to answer a question that every prospect has in her or his mind: Why should I come to *you* for that service? I am continually looking at every place where my business touches a prospect or a client to make sure that experience leaves them feeling wowed. When I wanted to add online booking, I evaluated many different systems to find the one that made the experience as seamless as possible for my clients.

When you discover what sets you apart, be sure that you remind yourself of it and your staff of it and that you act on it across the service experience. Be sure you are regularly communicating those differences in language that is easily understood by your clients and prospective clients.

Consider the touch points before, during, and after service. How well do you follow up with clients to make sure they are happy with the results? If you are committed to treating your clients like VIPs, how can you set yourself apart in every facet of the experience they have with you and your employees? Keep a sense of urgency in making your customer experience great.

At my spa, I have been successful enough marketing services that I have been able to double prices. I am not concerned that there are others in the same salon doing the same services because I am focused on creating a much better experience for my clients. When your book is too full, it is time to raise prices. Creating that level of demand is what you should aspire to achieve.

I use a variety of marketing methods. I use Facebook advertising, Facebook groups, and flyers. I also have a system that rewards current customers for referring friends and family. Whatever marketing you do, remember that every part of it is a reflection of you and your business.

When I first opened my business, I had a printer prepare some flyers for an upcoming event. The printer's work was sloppy and the finished flyer did not look like the proof. He wanted me to accept it, but I told him it had to be redone. Don't let anyone's sloppy work damage your brand. Insist on the best work from those who produce any of your marketing materials or anything else that your clients will see.

# CHAPTER 7

# KATIE GOFF
# OF WAVES SALON SERVICES

*"Pre-book! I pre-book 90 percent of my clients."*
—Stylist Katie Goff

I have been a stylist for 11 years. I spent the first part of my career as a salon employee. I had about two Saturdays off per year. Naturally, one of the things I like about being an independent professional is that it gives me the flexibility to design the life that I want. Right now, I am able to split my time between the United States and Mexico and have a balance to my life that makes me happier.

Stylist Katie Goff teaching a workshop

One of the keys to my success is that I pre-book everything.

When you are an independent operator, some days you will be busy and others not so much. Do all you can to make your daily revenue predictable by pre-booking as many of your clients as possible.

Splitting my time between the U.S. and Mexico actually makes it easier for me to pre-book clients because they want to get me while I am in the U.S. Even if you don't travel, think of reasons your clients should pre-book. For example, you might remind your client that the salon gets busy around back-to-school time, so pre-booking is a real advantage for them. I have gotten so that about 90% of my clients pre-book.

Think about the clients you do the best with and think about how to attract more of them. If your best clients are Junior Leaguers, consider volunteering at one of their charity events. If you want to attract students from a nearby college, go in with another salon pro and offer to do a night of hair and makeup tips for the members of a sorority on the eve of formal season.

Make sure that you consistently do excellent work so you are earning referrals. In this age of social media, however, it is also vital to gather feedback from every client and handle those who are dissatisfied promptly and fairly. Make sure the customers talking about you are the ones delighted with you and your service.

The reality is that being successful as an independent professional is not easy. It takes dedication and effort. When I went independent, I recognized I would be doing all of the things employees do in a commission-based salon and more. I expected to manage my book, to be accountable for selling product, and to be highly responsive to clients. As an independent, you should strive to respond to texts, phone calls, and emails during time between clients. Be responsive and have a sense of urgency in responding to your clients.

Marketing yourself may require you to go out of your comfort zone. If you are not okay talking to people about what you do for a living, you need to make yourself comfortable by doing it. The good news is the more you do it, the easier it gets. Make sure you have plenty of business cards whenever you go out.

Take pictures of your work to share on Instagram and Facebook. I have also had some success sharing my work on local Buy-Sell trade groups on Facebook. I have gotten paying clients and also done some trades for services. Try to find a new, low-cost place to advertise your business every week. Make sure you have a good online portfolio of your work. Many clients have ended up in my chair because they saw something I shared on Instagram. Being able to share a link to a page or two that shows a style a prospective client wants is a powerful way to get them to come in.

When you are on your own, you should not forget about continuing education. I budget for it like any other business expense. I also have found some wonderful ways to develop my skills. Many famous stylists share their work and how-tos on YouTube. I follow Jenny Strebe's *Confessions of Hairstylist* blog and am inspired by the work of other talented artists I find on Instagram. I attend at least one or two workshops per year to sharpen my skills.

# CHAPTER 8

# CHRISTINA LASATER

*"Being able to market yourself is THE crucial skill for independent salon pros."*
—Stylist Christina Lasater, Christina Lasater Studio

Stylist Christina Lasater

My name is Christina Lasater. I have owned Christina Lasater Studio at Salon & Spa Galleria in Fort Worth since January of 2016. I graduated from Ogle in Fort Worth in October of 2014. Although I had some good experiences working for salon owners and received some mentoring, not all of my experiences as a salon employee were good. I chose to open my own studio because I wanted to build a following for myself and be free to work with clients in my own way.

I am tuned in to my customers. I listen carefully and am meticulous about the notes that I keep about my clients and their preferences. Being extraordinarily client focused is partly why 90 percent of my clients followed me when I opened my studio.

Being able to market your services is THE crucial skill if you are going to be successful leasing salon space. Part of my success in this area comes from understanding what I do well. I am a reserved person. Some modes of in-person marketing, like talking with strangers at the grocery store, for example, are not a good fit for my personality. However, I know how to use social media and have used it effectively to get new clients. You should find ways to market yourself that fit you and make use of your talents.

Social media gives you an excellent opportunity to show results you have achieved. I take great care in getting quality before-and-after images of my work to share on Facebook and on Instagram. I regularly share new work and invite my clients to like and follow my pages. When I have a cancelation, I can often fill it by sharing the opening on social media. I have a system that allows me to automate posts so I keep my accounts fresh but can load a month's worth of posts at one sitting.

For services that take longer to perform, I take a credit card when I book the appointment. I charge a fee for no shows or cancellations without notice. While some clients balk at this, I have found it is a good way to ensure clients show up for their appointments. I work hard to ensure I am ready for the appointment and I get clients in my chair on time so they can plan their day accordingly. I don't eat unless that chair is full, so I have no problem charging clients who do not call and do not show up. You should develop a clear cancellation policy and be consistent in enforcing it.

One of the things I like best about having my own salon is the ability to experiment with different promotions and see what works. I try different promotions online and keep careful records so I know which ones are working and landing new people in my chair. I offer a discount on first services of 25% because I have found it helps to give people an incentive to try me. I advertise that offer on the back of my business card and online. I run promotions for Valentine's Day, Mother's Day, and other events.

Because I am focused on making every customer interaction as exceptional as possible, I earn a lot of business by referral. I have a program that rewards current clients with free services for recommending me to new clients. I give a free cut and style to anyone who sends me three new clients. This program has consistently been my best source of new business and has helped to convert some of my loyal clients into evangelists for my business.

Another key to my earnings has been my ability to pre-book the next appointment for my client. As I have gotten busier, I have found it is even easier to get clients to pre-book. I always phrase the request in a positive way and remind the client of the benefit of knowing when her or his next appointment will be. I usually simply ask the client which of two or three possible times is best for the appointment, rather than asking a yes-or-no question about whether they would like to book a next appointment.

I believe selling product is a great convenience for your clients and a good source of add-on income. My first foray into retailing products was with a product line I expected to sell more quickly than it did. While, I eventually sold through it, I recommend being conservative in buying product until you have a feel for the right level of inventory. Be careful about sinking too much cash into product inventory.

Getting my earnings to the level I wanted to achieve has taken longer than I expected as an independent professional. However, I have never been happier than I am today because I am in control of my business and am moving toward my goal of owning a salon with stylists working for me.

# CHAPTER 9

# KIMBERLY PELT
# OF KIM'S HAIR DESIGNS

*"Always show confidence to your clients."*

—Stylist Kimberly Pelt

Stylist Kimberly Pelt

My name is Kimberly Pelt, and I started my stylist career at age seventeen and became an independent stylist at eighteen. Several key factors have played a part in my success. A big part of my initial success was I learned early on not to let fear and uncertainty show. Any skill takes time and practice to master, but I always showed my confidence to my clients.

As a stylist, I have to have an open mind and to be willing to learn and to think outside the box. I keep in mind that I know more about what I'm doing than the client does. I have also invested the time to learn about new techniques and products.

In moments of uncertainty, I am not afraid to consult fellow stylists to get their outlook on what they would do or what products they would use. Throughout my career, I have committed myself to continue to be better.

Over my years, I have also learned the importance of location. A few times, in my early years, I moved to different salons in different cities. Although these locations were all within a thirty-minute drive, to some clients the extra travel time was a deal breaker.

Other clients followed me because they felt I was worth it. Eventually, I settled into an area and stayed. I have had a few more moves, but all of them have been within a two-mile radius.

The clientele I have grown comes from many different areas, but all of my clients are comfortable making the drive to see me. My advice is to make sure you choose an inviting location in a good neighborhood and stick with it.

Clients depend on me as a professional stylist to use the proper tools and products and to use only quality products. When it comes to the supplies a stylist can use, I have found you get what you pay for. Better quality products produce better, longer-lasting results.

Clients have many stylists to choose from and can even try over-the-counter products at home. I have always used the best salon-quality products because clients can see and feel the difference. Using better products means my clients look better and have healthier hair. Both make them happier and more likely to come back.

I feel the most important key to my success is building relationships and gaining my clients' trust. Staying confident and listening to what the clients want are two ways I build trusting relationships. That trust is what keeps clients coming back and telling their family, friends, and sometimes even strangers.

We all know women talk, and my clients are my walking-talking billboards! I learn my clients' needs, habits, and preferences. In return, I'm able to give my clients feedback about what they are telling me they want. Sometimes, what they want is not practical based on their hair type or habits. Clients respect that I can be honest with them and give them expert advice and options. I am always careful to ensure that I set realistic expectations with every client.

It is easy to build relationships with some clients. We just click. However, I would not be nearly as successful a stylist without working to build relationships when I *don't* click with the person in my chair. My philosophy is simple: I believe *everyone* who sits in my chair deserves to look and feel beautiful.

I have built many relationships that are still going strong, even with people I *don't* really click with. By building trusting relationships, I am able to keep more clients.

Every client interaction is important to me because word-of-mouth has always been my most effective means of advertising and growing my following. Obviously, it also takes talent to produce the results that each individual desires. Over my seventeen-year journey, I have tried a few different kinds of advertising, but word-of-mouth has produced the most consistent results.

I chose the path to lease as opposed to working on commission or for an hourly rate at a chain salon. As my own boss, I set my own hours and prices. I choose which products I want to use and which services I want to provide.

Being able to make these decisions allows me to have total freedom and control over my business and my income. Once the lease amount is made, the rest is mine, and the sky is the limit. I can work as much or as little as I would like.

Slaving away working for someone who tells me what to do, which products to use, when to work, which services I'm allowed to offer, all while taking most of the money I'm making is not my idea of using my full potential.

Sure, it's risky being self-employed; there are highs and lows. I only make money if there is a client in my chair. That is why it is so important to build those relationships and to remain positive through the tough times. My clients come to me because I can give them something they can't give themselves. That, in itself, is very rewarding.

By leasing my space, I have been able to express my talents freely, to reach my potential as a stylist, and to maximize my income.

# Chapter 10

# Ron's Sturgeon's Success Articles

*"We are what we repeatedly do. Excellence, then, is not an act, but a habit."*

—Will Durant

This chapter includes the most requested articles about success habits and business from Ron Sturgeon's popular monthly syndicated business advice column. Ron regularly writes for several business and trade publications. He has written hundreds of articles and eight popular books for business owners. You can learn more about him at his consulting website, MrMissionPossible.com.

Ron Sturgeon is Mr. Mission Possible

## TOOLS FOR SUCCESS — BE A PROMISE KEEPER

Always do EXACTLY what you say you will. People will learn that they can count on you, and you want that reputation. Don't make excuses. Just do what needs to be done.

When my partners and I sold GreenLeaf the second time, they gave me a Lucite trophy inscribed with the word *LOCKSMITH* because I was so good at unlocking the potential of people and getting the job done.

I can be a hard boss. However, people who have worked for me will tell you that they never had to wonder where they stood with me. I was honest in setting expectations, honest with how I would measure success, and honest with people about how they were performing. Those who could deliver, they excelled. Those who couldn't, they didn't stay long.

The people who work for you want the truth, and they will respect you for telling it. Of course, telling the truth does not mean telling all you know. When we bought GreenLeaf back from Ford, it was losing a million dollars per month. We had to decide which 300 people to let go. We knew who with some work, but we had good reasons not to tell until the time was right.

Remember that these situations are rare exceptions. You should strive to be direct and truthful with everyone in your business life. You never want to look back and wish you had just told the truth.

The truth can be painful, but, as my friend Don Egilseer used to say, it's an elixir. It can be healthy to get an issue out in the open where you and your employees can work on it. Did a customer write you a bad check, which caused your account to be overdrawn, and you then had a check returned? It's ok – call the person you gave the check to and explain what happened, how it's your responsibility, and tell them exactly how you will make it good.

If you can't deliver on ANY expectation, get in front of it, take ownership, don't whine or make excuses, and explain how you will make it right.

Part of being reliable in your business life is about what you promise. Don't take on projects you can't do. Don't overpromise. Always meet or exceed the deadlines you have agreed to.

If you find yourself always busting your hump to meet a promise that seems impossible the minute after you've said it, you need to rethink how you work. Yes, it's true that the people you promised appreciate your meeting the deadline, but they may not even notice how much blood and tears it cost you.

Be smarter. Give yourself a realistic deadline and those same people **will** notice you delivered sooner than you promised. You will be happier and you will reach your career goals sooner.

You should use the same thinking when you delegate tasks. Never give people on your project the REAL deadline. Always give a deadline that's BEFORE your true deadline so that you can still stay on track when someone else screws up.

One of my favorite sayings is "No one cares how bad the storm was; all they care about is whether you brought the ship in." When you're captain, make certain the ship gets there before you promised.

## TOOLS FOR SUCCESS — HAVE A MANTRA OF CONSTANT DEVELOPMENT AND IMPROVEMENT

**Read a business-building book per month**. Dog-ear pages, make notes, make sure you have takeaways, executable ideas. We all start at the same place. Some of us expand, and others don't. And, some of us who expand, keep expanding until we can't anymore. That's *can't*, not *won't*.

If you read eight best sellers about marketing, you will be 80 percent as smart as the marketing people who want to get paid for advice to help you. The same applies to other areas of knowledge that are vital to your business success. Read in those areas, especially the ones you feel least confident about.

After you finish a book, give it to your management team with the sections you have highlighted and pages you have dog-eared.

**Attend seminars focused on making your business grow.**
You should go to at least six per year in the early years. Your
team leaders should go with you. Some seminars will be
suited for owners or top financial managers, such as how to
minimize taxes. Other seminars, such as how to lead teams,
will be a good fit for many of your managers and team
leaders. There are one-day seminars on a host of valuable,
business-building topics: managing difficult personalities,
motivating salespersons, how to hire and fire, etc.

**Be passionate and have a sense of urgency about using
what you learn.** Be sure that what you learn gets translated
into plans that make your business measurably better. Last
month's article was about how to make the transition from
boss to leader. Being passionate and a having a sense of
urgency about winning in business is part of making that
jump.

**Cultivate positive dissatisfaction.** My good friend Dixon
Thayer, former CEO at GreenLeaf, had a saying I still
use and love. He used to tell me always to have positive
dissatisfaction. Positive dissatisfaction requires you to
always be learning and expecting more, but also to always
be positive as you reach a succession of higher goals.

**Capture the motivating power of team training.** I have
found that seminars and trainings are one of the best ways
to motivate your most valuable people. Pay attention to
how team members respond to the opportunity to go get
new skills. Some won't want to go. They may still be solid
employees but they may be left behind because they don't
get the skills needed to take your business to where you
intend it to go.

Remember your best people will be motivated by the opportunity to acquire new skills or hone existing ones. Your accounting staff, for example, will be energized when you send them to an advanced excel class. Make sure you display the certificates they have earned. Be sure to recognize staff members who make exceptional use of their new skills in meeting your business goals.

Ron Sturgeon on CNBC's *Blue Collar Millionaires®*

## TOOLS FOR SUCCESS — BE TECHNOLOGICALLY SAVVY

In 1992, before Smartphones existed, I carried a Pocket Rolodex everywhere I went. I did it because I understood the value of networking, and I put EVERYONE'S information in my rolodex. I never entered a person's information without including their full address and phone. We didn't have e-mail then.

Most of my friends made fun of me for being the nerd with the Rolodex. However, they all also relied on me for phone numbers. In 1999, when I did a private stock offering, I had over 3,000 contacts that I had gathered and put in my pocket Rolodex because I had networked or done business with them.

Using just that list, I was able to sell out my private stock offering in 21 days. In fact, I actually attracted more investors than I had stock to sell. I'm sharing this story partly to remind you to network. But that's not the only reason.

I'm also sharing it to remind you to keep your tech skills up-to-date. Can you build a simple spreadsheet? Use PowerPoint? Upload to SlideShare? Draft a letter in Word or edit a document using track changes? Convert a doc to a PDF? Manage your e-mail and docs so you work smart? As a leader, you should know all of these basic tech skills.

Stay current. Get ahead of the curve. Go to seminars. Learn about Search Engine Optimization (SEO). Understand how to use private groups on Facebook to sell more to current customers. You don't have to be a web genius to try new tools.

Abe Lincoln once said, "Give me six hours to chop down a tree, and I will spend the first four sharpening my axe." He knew how important tools are to doing the job right. Investing time to upgrade your skills is sharpening your axe. Work at mastering new tools and new skills.

If you drive a forklift or work with your hands, this week's article is for you, too. If you want to do better for yourself and make more money, you need to learn skills that will make you more valuable. You become promotable by looking for areas that the business needs help and learning the skills needed to give it.

Volunteer to learn new skills, whether it is learning to control inventory, make presentations, work on a budget, understand metrics, or review contracts. Add any of these marketable skills, and it won't be long until your paycheck reflects your higher value.

The pocket Rolodex is long gone. Today, I use an iPhone. I network on Facebook and LinkedIn. I study online marketing. I am nearly 60, but I'm still eager to find new tools to make me a better businessperson.

## TOOLS FOR SUCCESS — KEEP PERFECT CREDIT

When I got in business, I had no money. I borrowed nearly every penny to start my first business. I became pretty darn good at borrowing money. I was one of the first auto recyclers to borrow large sums to buy cars, a feat that many people in the business believed to be impossible.

The key to getting my banker to say yes was cultivating a relationship. If you want to know step-by-step how to build a solid relationship that will let you get the capital you need, buy my book, *Getting to Yes with Your Banker,* on Amazon.

For now, let me share a little about the importance of having good credit. To a banker, there is no substitute for good credit.

How do you keep good credit?

One of the crucial steps is to protect yourself from identity theft and credit fraud. Make sure you have a watch on your credit report. All the credit bureaus offer them. Credit monitoring service is not expensive. It costs about $14 per month and is an absolute must. Having a watch on your file means that the bureaus will alert you whenever anyone accesses your credit file and whenever your credit score changes.

You should also check the accuracy of the information in your credit file. Order a tri-bureau (one that covers all three credit bureaus) report with scores. Be proactive in removing any inaccurate derogatory information.

Is your score at least a 720? If it isn't, you need to think about how to get it there. A 720 is the current cut off for prime loans. If your score is at least a 720, your past credit history will not be the reason your loan application is turned down.

Once you know where you stand and have a program to keep an eye on your credit reports, you need to be diligent about keeping promises to your creditors. If you can't pay a credit card in full, pay the minimum due and PAY IT ON TIME. Yes, it was only ten dollars, but it's the promise you kept, not the amount you paid, that matters.

My credit file has records dating back to 1979. It's perfect. Not one payment was ever late. That's the sort of reassurance bankers like. They like a sterling credit report much better than a story. Bankers don't have time for stories. They care about results. Be known as the client who moves fast, handles his business, and stays in front of issues. My bankers love me because I'm credible, entertaining, and VERY candid. I call it like it is. They can count on my results.

The other reason that bankers love me is that they make a lot of money on me. When I come to them for money, I have a very profitable use for it, and I know that a quarter or a half point won't make any difference to the quality of my life or my business. I act accordingly.

I don't try to beat every banker out of every quarter point. I want them to point at me when I come in the lobby and say, "There goes one of our best customers. We make a lot of money on him."

If you do your job right and make a strong application for a loan (one that has solid answers to the what, why, how, etc.), banks will likely want your business enough to give you a competitive rate. If they don't, ask them to review the rate.

However, think beyond the one transaction. Think long term. Build a relationship with your bankers. Notice I said *bankers*. I always have two. Having two lets the banker you are talking to know that he or she has potential competition.

A little *potential* competition is good for the heart and good for the relationship. Stay tuned for more on good credit and how to keep it in next month's article.

## TOOLS FOR SUCCESS –
## PERFECT CREDIT PT 2 – BANKING SMART

The first article in this series listed several tactics to increase your business success. Each of the successive articles takes a closer look at one of those tactics. Last month, we talked about the importance of keeping perfect credit and building long-term banking relationships.

No matter what anyone else tells you, ALWAYS have and use two banks. Have a business bank and a personal bank, or mix it up. No matter how you do it, you must have loans at two banks to keep your bankers on their toes.

What kind of banks should you work with? Don't choose a large national bank. Instead, find a local community bank. Every area has at least two and most areas have several strong community banks. These banks typically have less than 500-million in assets, but the very largest community banks may have as much as one billion.

Open a checking account to begin your relationship with the bank. You need to have a separate business account in any case. Ask your banker what the bank's loan-to-deposit ratio is. He or she will be thrilled you are informed enough to want to know.

Here's why you need to know. As a practical matter, banks don't loan more than 80% of the value of their deposits. That means a bank with $100-million in deposits and 75- to 80-million in loans isn't going to approve your loan PERIOD. On the other hand, a bank with a loan-to-deposit ratio of 60% is likely to welcome your loan application.

Do you see why having two banks is so important? If you have only one banking relationship, you may need money when your bank isn't inclined to lend because of its loan-to-deposit ratio.

The loan mix in a bank's portfolio can also affect your likelihood of getting a loan. Banks love to do loans for owner-occupied residential real estate, but they may be less open to a particular kind of loan if they feel they have too much density in that kind of loan at the time you're asking. If you have the right relationship, your banker should be willing to tell you when loan density is affecting decisions.

When you are applying for a loan, NEVER allow a banker to check your credit until you are ready. Instead, bring your banker a credit report with tri-bureau scores when you discuss the loan. If you decide to go ahead, your banker can pull a report to approve your loan. In the meantime, however, you won't damage your score with too many inquiries.

In addition, if you have to go to a different bank, your second bank will not immediately see that you were just across the street trying to get a loan. Protect your credit score and your privacy by being smart about when you let a banker run your credit.

Ron Sturgeon, his beloved Cavaliers, and Ford GT

## TOOLS FOR SUCCESS –
## BE YOUR OWN ADVOCATE – NO ONE ELSE WILL

One of the first lessons I learned in business was to be assertive in promoting myself. When I'm successful, I talk about it. I am also willing to share what I have learned from a long career in business as a mentor. In business as in life, you will find that what goes around comes around. Your reputation as a helper of other businesspeople will be remembered and repaid in ways you cannot foresee.

However, know that when you begin to promote yourself, you will find that some peers will resent you for doing it. Don't let that stop you. They are a minority. Don't let them deprive you of opportunities by creating too much anxiety about what others think.

Years ago, Donald Trump spoke about this at a seminar I attended. Yes, he's polarizing, but he is not shy about promoting himself and has been very successful as a result. If you get nothing else from this article, remember this: No one is going to be your advocate; you must do it yourself.

If you don't tell your story, who will know when you do charitable things? When you do innovative things? When you achieve new milestones? When your business gets so successful you have to hire new staff or give a star in your organization greater responsibility? All these events are newsworthy, whether you share them in an employee newsletter or send out a press release.

You do have a news mailing list, right? This would be key business contacts, bankers, and close friends. You should be gathering contacts and networking continually, but if you want to start on a small non-computerized scale, take a sheet of mailing labels and handwrite labels for the key people.

Now when you have news, a new brochure, anything (try to mail something at least quarterly), copy the labels in your copy machine and slap them on some envelopes. I maintain my list on my iPhone, syncing with Outlook, and have over 3,000 contacts divided into categories like business, personal, news, etc. I can output and create labels in a minute.

How are people to know if you don't tell them? Make sure you add your bankers to your good- news mailing list; they will love getting news about your business and sharing it will strengthen your relationship. Most business owners don't make a habit of sharing successes with their bankers, and so they miss a chance to show how "on it" they are.

You have a lot more news opportunities than you think. Just added a new service? Added a new employee? Promoted someone to a management position? Put a new quality control system in place? (Even if it sounds simple to you, it sounds great to others, and can even become part of a unique selling proposition).

My girlfriend sells insurance and uses events to connect with prospects. (We have co-written a book about how to use events to grow your business. You can find it on my web site or amazon). Because of the events, she routinely has customers come to her and say, "I feel like I know you. I see your name all over town." This HAS TO BE GOOD for business. When you are out telling your story, sharing, and mentoring, customers feel connected with you and that connection will lead them to you when they need what you sell.

Even a carefully chosen failure and the lessons you learned from it can be part of your story. Don't be afraid to speak at the local Lions Club about your success or something innovative about your business. Ask to speak to budding entrepreneurs at the local high school or college. To them, your real-world experience is much more interesting than a textbook or journal article by a Ph.D.

And, yes, that speaking engagement is newsworthy; your banker respects those who give back. Your employees will love a boss who is a mentor. By the way, the public speaking will also make you much better at leading when it counts.

## TOOLS FOR SUCCESS – LEARN MARKETING AND ADVERTISING

Learn marketing and advertising. Of course, you need good products and services, but without good marketing you will likely underachieve or even fail. Know your customers. Have a unique selling proposition. Make the customer king; be sincere and passionate about it. If you aren't a creative marketer, find someone to help you in this area.

Who are your customers? What is your unique selling proposition? What makes you different from your competitors? Can you articulate it in writing? They don't want to hear rhetoric like our quality is higher. Even in the rare cases when a quality claim is true, today's consumers are jaded. They are skeptical of claims that don't come with some proof.

What could you do differently to show you are better than your competition in ways that matter? Do you offer evening and weekend appointments? Do you offer mobile service? Do you guarantee your work? Do you offer touch up service if your client stops in between regular visits?

Whatever the promise you make to your clients, mean it. Walk it. Train it. Breathe it. Believe it. Empower your people to make the customer happy. Make sure that the experience in your chair is always better than you promised.

## TOOLS FOR SUCCESS — HAVE A SENSE OF URGENCY

There is no substitute for an EXTREME sense of urgency. Don't wait to do it, do it now! Delegate it! Make it happen! You know already intuitively that no matter how fast you move in the world of business it's not fast enough. Practice the urgency every day. Every week. Every month. Be tireless; make sure everyone around you knows that you always wanted it yesterday. Their sense of urgency leverages on yours.

Why wait months to get a new marketing design? Do it this week. Why wait to shake down the reason for high expenses in your service department? Do it today, get started, ask someone for all the metrics and reports for your review by this Thursday!

Make sure that you delegate effectively, as there are many tasks that you may not need to do at all, or have others gather information so you can make a decision.

Many of you want better profits. The path to profits requires a big sense of urgency to achieve it and stay ahead of your competitors. How do you do that? It's simple; insist on your preliminary financial statements absolutely no later than the 10th. Ignore those who tell you it's not possible, we had to close the books and publish them by the 5th, regardless of weekends and holidays! Why? Because AS SOON AS YOU GET IT, on THAT morning, study it. Make sure it shows the prior 12 months (so it covers 13 months, including the same month last year). Study it for changes, comparing to the prior month and same month last year.

Shine your mental "flashlight" on several items that are either up or down, and MARCH right out of your office to that department. Get details. Ask the accounting dept. to explain why utility bills doubled last month, and why brokered parts sales are off 30% for the last 3 months. Schedule a meeting TOMORROW with the sales staff to discuss how to get brokered parts sales up. Figure out who is leaving all the fans on in the shop, install thermostats on the HVAC system that cuts it off at night. (We use Nest thermostats).

Now smile and go back to work. You have had an impact on THIS month's sales, the month right after the statement you studied. If you don't get your statement until later in the month, or even the next month and then delay reviewing it, then procrastinate on taking steps, it's easy to see that you won't impact things for many months, so it will only make a difference maybe 3 times per year.

Imagine how fast things will change if you shine that flashlight on just 2 items per month. That's 24 initiatives per year. One of my favorite sayings is, "Where you check and shine your flashlight, you get improvement."

Do you have a way to track the efficacy of your buyer's purchases? Metrics that measure how quickly the inventory turns? (I see a lot of heads turning side to side). DO you know that it has been proven repeatedly that purchases that do the best in the first month do the best in the long term? Getting in front of bad purchasing is one of the quickest ways to increase cash flow and profits. Put the system in place now and start meeting with the buyer regularly, at least monthly.

**DO IT TODAY**. Bad employee? Get to work moving them out. Do everything sooner rather than later. It can be exhausting for your staff, but they also will respect what you are and do, employees love being part of success.

Consultant Ron Sturgeon advising business owners

## TOOLS FOR SUCCESS – DON'T BE AFRAID TO BE A REBEL

Don't be afraid to be a rebel – Push back, think out of the box, but be strategic and analytic about it. You don't have to be combative to be a rebel. Think innovative. Think doubting and questioning the establishment. Think positive energy. Think unexpected. Think passionate. And yes, at times it can be lonely being a rebel.

It can also be fun. I was always trying new things. I attended the trade shows for collision repairers to find innovative new ways they were working. New tools, new marketing methods. I knew they were ahead of us. And it couldn't hurt to understand their business better.

I was carrying an electronic organizer in 1990, and was the first to carry a brick phone in 1990. But you don't have to be bleeding edge in technology to stay ahead. We bought Apple IIe's to computerize our inventory, and there was no software to do that, but I knew it would save time.

I was reading a book per month, and learning things about business that just weren't normal in our industry, even though they were commonplace in other industries. I was the first to put salespersons on commissions, though other industries had been doing it for decades. At the time, in 1985, any decent counterperson wanted $1,000 in cash per week, with no regard for how much they sold.

I was new in the industry, so doubted almost everything I heard, and wasn't afraid to try something that worked in another industry in our industry.

I spoke at conventions, and many thought what I was sharing was intended to mislead them, as no one could possibly be willing to share that much info. I got what I gave, and many shared with me. One benefit to speaking is that you become a much better leader, and your communication skills are much improved.

I never fussed about things I couldn't control. Many were unhappy about new competitors at the auction, and were quick to tell newbies that they weren't allowed to bid on all cars. I thought that was crazy, and they tried to make me pay too much for cars, to "teach me a lesson". I just ignored them. Copart actually asked me to come to some of their out of town auctions to disrupt bid rigging, as they knew I would bid what the cars were worth to me. They gave me deals on storage since I was buying out of town, which was very unorthodox. I was working 20 auctions per week, and had gobs of desirable inventory, while others just worked locally and had to pay too much or not get the inventory they wanted.

I was advertising out of my area, and tracking results. Inc. Magazine in 1996 wrote me up for innovative tracking methods of calls, prospects, and customers. I remember that in 1986 I got a call from an angry recycler in Pennsylvania. He said, "Don't be mailing things to my customers here. If they need a Mercedes engine, they will call me, and I can call you." WOW. He was old school, and I was the rebel for sure.

I was always positive, which is a bit different. My dad taught me that no one gives a crap if your feet hurt, so don't bother telling them about it. Those who know me know how I answer when you ask me how I am doing. I always say *the best*. Being positive surprises people and makes you stand out because so few people are.

One cautionary note. Many issues you will face have established best practices. Don't be so innovative that you overlook doing those fundamentals, which I call blocking and tackling. Be sure to keep doing all that blocking and tackling while you innovate.

I often find folks looking for the latest gee-whiz stuff to make their business better, when they aren't doing the basics. A good example is a business owner that wants to start using Twitter, but he hasn't updated his web site in 5 years. Everyone tells him Twitter is the hottest new thing. Twitter is an incremental tool and is not likely to affect your business in a material way.

## Tools for Success – Watch and Understand Your Competitors, But Focus on Building Your Business

As business owners, sometimes we become obsessed with what our competitors are doing. Don't misunderstand. Of course, you do need to understand your competitors and pay attention to them, but that does not mean you need to respond to everything they do. Nor should you ever let concern about them stop you from building your business. Sometimes, however, you do need to get data about competitors.

Not long ago, I was starting a new venture, renting salon suites and chairs to beauty professionals, and I needed to understand what competitors were doing to make sure that I entered the market with the right value propositions.

I could have hired a high-priced consultant and gotten the information I needed. Instead, I wrote an advertisement, placed it on craigslist, and found a retired businessperson with a market research background to help me do a focused competitor study. This person cost $15 per hour and was delighted to help with the project.

We started by mystery shopping the competitors, both on the phone and in-person. We gathered all of the results in a spreadsheet and a short report. For less than $2,000, I was able to learn a great deal about all of the Tarrant County salons renting spaces or suites.

I got copies of their leases, found out their rates, learned whether they provided towels, and discovered whether they charged tenants for washers and dryers. The study also showed me which of my competitors offered tenants free Wi-Fi and provided the answers to a litany of other specific questions about the competition.

With this data, I was able to build my value propositions in ways that make my salons more attractive to beauty professionals wanting to rent space. I learned what to do and, as important, what not to do by having the researcher do mystery shops and talk to leasing professionals and operators during site visits.

I knew the approximate size of the competitors' operations from tax records and site visits, about how many vacancies they had, and what they were charging for rent. In some cases, I even heard which tactics they were using to find tenants. What people will tell you if you ask amazes me.

When I was running an auto-salvage yard, I periodically mystery shopped my competitors because I wanted to know how we compared on metrics that matter. I gathered data on how long it took my competition to answer the phone.

I sent someone to buy a small part so that I could see how the warranty each competitor offered compared with ours. I looked to see how neat their operations appeared. I gathered data to estimate sales volume and sales-per-employee, key performance indicators for salvage yards.

Another easy, low-cost way to monitor competitors is to set up a Google alert on their company name (easy to do at google.com/alerts). If they have an e-mailed newsletter for customers offered on their website, sign up so that you can see what they are sending to customers and how often.

I watched my competitors, but I did not obsess over them. I didn't do something just because a competitor started doing it. More often, because I was peer benchmarking with non-competitive yards in other markets, I was the most innovative local yard. If you are interested in learning how to use this technique, I have written about it in *Peer Benchmarking Groups: One Entrepreneur's Story of Extreme Success.*

Because I was leading the way, competitors had to decide whether to respond. Yes, I had an eye on them, but I didn't let them worry me much. I stayed too busy planning, managing, measuring, and executing. You should too.

## TOOLS FOR SUCCESS — POSITIVE ENERGY — THE WAY TO THE TOP

Those of you who know me know I live the positive energy mantra. What do I say when you ask me how I am doing? I say, "The **best!**" There is no other way to achieve maximum success in what can be the grueling drive to the top.

How can you practice positive energy? What will practicing it do for you?

- **Even in the middle of something negative, you can be positive**. Look for that path, live it, breathe it, and evangelize it. Everyone around you will notice and positive energy makes whatever you are facing likely to come out better. An employee wrecked the delivery truck this morning? He's ok, and we needed to replace that truck anyway. Now we can get the larger model, and aren't we glad we had insurance! Rent a truck and move on.

- **Always be cheerful**. My dad taught me that no one cares if your feet hurt, so why tell them! Being positive is infectious and appreciated by those around you most of the time.

- **Positive energy can get you and your team through a rough spot; just keep it positive!** Again, your team will notice and be more effective.

- **You can usually find a positive result, even in a bad financial report**. You still have to work on the bad fundamentals, but approach them with a positive spin. In other articles, I've talked about my old boss at Ford, Dixon Thayer, and his mantra of *positive dissatisfaction*. Being positive will bring better results; no one likes to have negative energy.

- **In private meetings, even when admonishing employees, get past the admonishment as soon as possible and focus on the path forward with a program to solve the issue and get to the result you both want**. The employee wants to get through it more than you, and leaving it on a positive note can get the employee over the negative feelings sooner. When you have to do one of those sessions, give the employee time and space to lick their wounds.

- **With vendors, bankers, and other stakeholders, you want to be the one they remember as always having positive energy.** Be careful not to be unrealistically optimistic so that you can always under promise and over deliver.

- **Using the same positive energy in your personal life will improve your home life and your relationship with your kids and spouse.**

Don't confuse having positive energy with just sugar coating everything negative. Not holding others or yourself accountable is not positive energy. Nor does positive energy mean you are unrealistically optimistic. Just be happy and optimistic as you plow through the minutia of the grind to the top. And love what you do.

You can't fake positive energy for more than a short time; you have to adopt it, and be bought in and you must love what you do (most of the time). If you don't love what you do, go find something else that you want to do enough to let the positive energy flow.

## Tools for Success — Do The Hard Stuff First!

When faced with a difficult task, too often, we procrastinate. Putting off hard tasks is costly. It kills work ethic, lowers productivity, and reduces urgency. Worst of all, it delays the day when the hard task will be done.

Think for a moment about your business. Is there a task you dread? Is there something you put off when you get to your office? Whether you're putting off a small daily task or a major undertaking, I have advice for you.

If it is a small daily task, do the thing you dread most first. When I came to work, I made it a rule to do what I least wanted to do first. After I had that must-do task done, I got momentum because I could devote the rest of the day to doing work that I liked better.

If the task that you least want to do is a big job or project, take a few minutes and list the steps needed to complete it. Once you have reduced the elephant to bite-sized pieces, take a bite, first thing every day, before you move on to the rest of your to-do list.

As you look at the project or major job, you may find that there are parts of it that a team member can do for you. If possible, delegate them to the person or the people who can do them better than you can. If you cannot delegate them, do whatever is next on that project first.

Most of the time, you will find that the task is not as bad as you imagined it would be. And, you can redirect the energy you were devoting to procrastinating and worrying to serving your customers, growing your revenues, and increasing your profits.

Whenever I think about procrastination, I think of an employee I had. I nicknamed him Motorcycle Craig because, whenever he had to start a job, he acted like a little man on a tiny motorcycle at the foot of Mount Everest. He buzzed back and forth. He told anyone who would listen, "I can't do it; I can't do it." He would do anything not to have to start a job.

Once he started, however, he found he could do the job much better than he expected. You can be more productive and enjoy your work more starting today. Do the small task you dread most first. If it's a big project you're putting off, take a step toward completing it first thing every day.

I talk about to-do lists in another article in this series. Successful people make to-do lists. I still make one nearly every day. Sometimes, I estimate the time each item will take so I can get a snapshot of my day. Whether you include time estimates or not, make the first item on your to-do list your least favorite must-do item.

If you hate to review financial statements, make sure your bookkeeper leaves them on your desk before he or she goes home so that you can look at them when you are the freshest. Hate email? Do it first and then close it. Now go have fun! Remember to have positive energy, channel your positive dissatisfaction, and maintain your strong sense of urgency.

Serial Entrepreneur and Consultant Ron Sturgeon

## TOOLS FOR SUCCESS — KEEP SHOOTING THE GUN

A competitor told me to keep shooting the gun when I had only been in business a few years. I wasn't the brightest, and I certainly didn't have any money. I had to keep up the pace! I was also the youngest and most inexperienced. Walter Williams, an old salvage friend and mentor said, "It's hard to stay ahead of you, Sturgeon; you work all the time and never stop shooting the gun."

That was 35 years ago, but what he said stuck with me. I respected my competitors, and knew hard work was the only way I was going to best the others. While they were in *Cancun* or fishing, I was reading a book on marketing or studying the most recent financials for opportunities to improve.

Not long ago, I was mentoring a young friend, and he asked me what was the single most important thing I could teach him as he starts the journey to success. I told him to read a book a month, and gave him three to read. He's bright, and not lazy, but a year later, he hasn't finished the books. It's clear that his priorities are elsewhere.

Another article in this series speaks to having a sense of urgency, a related topic. My mentee will do ok, maybe even well. But he won't do *great*. He won't be an innovator or leader in his industry. And he won't be able to keep a mentor because he does not follow the easy steps that precede the valuable learning.

When I heard Walter tell me to keep shooting the gun, I had noticed that many of my competitors who had been in business a few years seemed to take a lot of time off. They were resting on their laurels. I was hungry.

Let me add a qualification here for those who don't want to be an over achiever. There's not a thing wrong with that. If your dream of success is a 2-year-old BMW, a nice brick home, a lovely wife and 3 well dressed and educated kids, and never missing a soccer game, figure out what that means financially. When you get there, lay the gun down. Unless a taste of success has made you want to have a little more.

## Tools for Success – Successful People Make Lots of Lists

Are you a list maker? Try not to make too much fun of the person with a bunch of lists! Many studies have concluded that successful people make lots of lists.

Here are some kinds of lists you should make to be more productive:

- **Daily to do list** - Yes, it may be almost the same as yesterday's list, but it refocuses and reprioritizes your day. Sometimes. I even put the amount of time by each item that I think it will take, so I have an idea how realistic the list is. Sometimes, I number items on the list or color code them, for priority. If I have a *stick-in-the-spokes* deadline, I circle it or make sure it's first in line. As I work through the list, I even remind myself that I can't go to lunch until I do that hot item. Yes, I give myself rewards. Another article in the series talks about doing the hardest or most distasteful stuff first, a good technique when you can reshuffle because it lets you face the hard stuff with peak energy.

- **A master to do list** - The dream list, everything but the kitchen sink. Things like working on my will. Who wants to do that? But you do have to get to it eventually, so having it on a master list makes me think about it.

- **My MBWA list** - Manage-by-Walking-Around list. I keep it in my phone. People think "Jeez, he never misses anything!" No I'm not smarter and my memory isn't any better than most, but I write it all down. When I remember something I need to do or handle, I put it on that list.

- **Email List** - I have an app on my phone that with one button emails me. If I recall something I need to do, I email myself. This in conjunction with my policy of never deleting an email until it's handled – it gets things done. You young'uns will want to text yourself, but you're unlikely to refer to texts to recall stuff you need to get done.

- **Outlook List** - No, I guess it's not really a list. I use Microsoft Outlook's calendar to save reminders. When did you last change the batteries in your smoke detectors? When is your next oil change? When was your air compressor serviced? What about that loan maturity in 5 years? Will you wait until the bank notifies you, or start working on it 6 months in advance because it was in your reminders? And silly me, sometimes I snap a picture of the calendar item and e-mail it to myself. That assures me it's handled. More often than not, these items will be delegated via email, when I get to them in my inbox the next day.

The list of my lists goes on and on. I break big jobs into smaller steps, which are in a list. I am writing this article because it's in a list of articles that I keep adding to when I think of a topic.

And I know you love your computer and Excel, but sometimes a good old #2 pencil and a Big Chief tablet are still the best way to get a list going. Or *Post-It* notes! If you wait until you are in front of your computer to add to a list, you forget half of it.

## Tools for Success —
## Never Underestimate the Value of an Hour

Time, our most precious commodity. There never seems to be enough. However, maybe there is more time than we think? Don't think about your time in hours. Think minutes. Even seconds. How do we gain a few extra minutes here and there?

- **Delegate** - I know, I know, you can do it in the time it takes to delegate it. That's likely true on the first time and half true the second time. There are things we can delegate that will save 10 minutes a day. But we won't invest the 30 minutes it takes to teach someone else to do them. Maybe even a few teaching sessions. So that failure on our part costs us 10 minutes a day **FOR THE REST OF OUR LIVES.** That's many 10-minute segments, folks. Think about EVERYTHING you do. Could someone else do it with some training? You will be surprised how many things you will find to delegate.

- **Kick your inner perfectionist to the curb** - I know, you think no one else can do it as well as you. You are likely completely correct. But if they can do it 90% as well, that's good enough. If it will free you to do more important things, then it's a win. Stop being a perfectionist. Competitors used to ask me, "Sturgeon, how can you find 150 employees you can tolerate, and I can't find 5?" I tell them to look in the mirror; it's all about hiring, training, mentoring, leading, and, err, err, tolerating *mediocrity*. I know it's an ugly word, but let's keep it *real* folks, not everyone is equally smart, skilled, qualified or experienced. Get over it.

- **Know the answer to this question** - What is your time worth? It's not the same for everyone. But there is a number at which you can hire someone to do your job as well as you do, or it's what you charge the company for your services, or it's what you want to make. It's more than $10-$20 per hour for sure! Now, why did you stay home to wait for the cable repair guy last Thursday, missing 3 hours of work? Why are you washing your truck? Think big to do big. Hire others to do things you *shouldn't, can't* or *won't* do. Now there's a catch here, you don't do this so you can play golf, generally. REALLY use the expensive time. Study your financials, work on the marketing plan, go through the bids for new equipment, or maybe work on your will! (Yes, it was in another article in this series about keeping lists, and prioritizing, and as bad as it sounds, working on your will, which you simply haven't had time to do, is more important than washing your truck.)

If you use the tools here I've discussed, I guarantee you can find an hour per day. That's 5 hours per week, and 260 hours per year that can be used to make you smarter, more effective, and likely make you more satisfied with what you get done daily, and then HAPPIER!

## TOOLS FOR SUCCESS — GET WEB SMART

The first article in this series listed more than 25 tactics to increase your business success. I have used all of them. I started with nothing. I didn't get to college, so I know you can achieve maximum success, regardless of your level of education. E-mail me to get the first or any of the other articles in the series. Each one after the first takes a closer look at one of the tactics.

How are you using the web to ensure that people using search engines to find parts find you and your business? My experience tells me that me that many yard owners still have a simple web site, one that was done on the cheap by their nephew. Most owners know that they should have the website redone, but it is not a high priority.

If that's your story, you probably have a website that is not getting much traffic from search engines. That's a costly mistake. Make having your business site redone a priority. Work with a person with knowledge of search engine optimization (SEO).

If you would like to see how close your current design is to being SEO friendly, send me an email with your business websites URL and I will send you a free SEO audit report on your site. Please put free SEO audit in the subject line of your e-mail.

In the meantime, here are ten things you should be doing to get more business from your website:

- You should have a list of key words that you want to "own" for your area. You should know the keywords. When someone types these words into Google, you need to appear near the top of the results. You should be looking at a monthly report to see how well your marketing efforts are working and to see how far you have moved up or down in the results for keywords.

- You should be using the keywords or terms in the text and titles for pages on your site. You should have pages with titles that match the valuable terms.

- You should be using relevant keywords in your Craig's list ads and all other places that you are sharing content on the web. Make sure your eBay listings are helping your SEO by putting relevant keywords in them and giving them good titles.

- You should have videos posted that include keywords to make sure they are found and lead potential customers back to your site and you.

- You should issue periodic press releases using the keywords. Put a link on the keyword and point it back at the page for that keyword on your site. I like a service called 24-7 Press releases for these.

- You should be using the keywords on Twitter, Facebook, and other social site where you have content.

- You should make sure that your site displays properly on mobile devices. Can someone using a

smart phone or tablet to browse your inventory find
what they want and order it easily?

- Make sure your site has a large prominent button
  that says "FIND PARTS" on the home page. Folks
  came to buy something. Don't make them scroll
  past pics of your yard and verbiage. Make it easy for
  visitors to find the parts they came to buy.

- Stop scrimping on the site. Your nephew is a sweet
  kid, but a good site done by an SEO pro will start
  at around $3,000. Most web designers say they
  understand SEO, but they really don't, so seek out
  an expert on SEO. Be more focused on visibility and
  usability than on how pretty or slick it looks.

- You do not need pay per click (PPC) to be
  successful. Paying for visitors is a lazy man's way to
  find limited success. It is a costly way to compensate
  for a crappy non-SEO-optimized site with no
  supporting strategy. Relying on PPC will cause you
  to spend $500 or $1,000 a month forever because
  you would not spend $6,000 the first year and much
  lower ongoing costs.

A robust web strategy is necessary if you want to get your
small business to maximum success. Starting on yours will
put you ahead of some of your competitors. One of my
consulting practices is helping business owners use the web
to generate leads and sales. In many of my own ventures,
we rely on traffic from search engines and SEO to ensure
prospective clients find us. We own top positions for our
keywords. You can too.

## TOOLS FOR SUCCESS – BUILDING A NETWORK LIST

The first article in this series listed more than 25 tactics to increase your business success, all of them based on my experience. I started with nothing and didn't get to college, so I know you can achieve maximum success, regardless of your education. E-mail me to get the first article (or any of the other articles) in the series. Each takes a closer look at one of the tactics listed in that first article.

I know this sounds trivial, but it has to be in the top-10-most-important secrets of my success. You see, no matter how smart you are or how hard you work, you simply can't achieve maximum success without help. Many of my articles talk about how you need others to help you, using leverage, delegating, being efficient, on and on. Many of those tactics require mastering this seemingly trivial tactic.

When I was 30, I was saving business cards. I started using a pocket electronic rolodex in the 80s, and everyone made fun of me for it. This was long before iPhones or PDAs (Can you say Treo or Palm?). If you had a lake house, I knew the phone number. I was everyone else's phone directory. All my friends used to say, "Sturgeon's got the number; ask him."

I'm not sure when I truly realized the value of keeping a database of contacts, sometime in the 90's I reckon, I just knew it made me more efficient and saved me time (another article in this series covers tactics to find an extra hour per day). I had a protocol for entering contacts though. I always entered your full name, phone, and mailing address. And keywords. This was important. If I met you at a business meeting, I got your card and entered what you did, and keywords like *met at Kiwanis Club May 1993*.

When I did my first private stock offering I had over 2,000 contacts. Today, its 4,000. Today, I put them in categories also, for further sorting. It takes me a minute or so, but it has paid off in spades. Need an SBA loan consultant? I've got 3 in my phone. Plumber? I can type the word plumber in the keywords, and 12 of those folks pop right up. I recently had a friend hit a young boy on a bicycle and kill him. He needed a criminal attorney. I've never needed one but had 3 referrals to offer my friend. The list goes on and on. I use the list. If you and I were business friends, you would regularly hear from me by mail. Today, I email mostly but the principle of building a contact list is the same.

I've got every reporter who ever wrote a story about me. Every banker that I met or who has made me a loan. Every attorney, real estate professional, and folks that do obscure things like land survey, phase-one environmental reports, CAD drawings, or transportation cost audits. Imagine all the folks you've met that you later you wished you could remember when the time comes.

Today, it's about email. In a flash, as fast as you can say *keep a list*, I can reach out to that guy I met 5 years ago who does asbestos remediation reports. That's efficient! I just scan my Outlook contacts for the word *asbestos* and I am on it!

Now, about that stock offering. They say one out of 10 private stock offerings gets to document stage, and one out of 50 actually funds. That's one-in-500 odds. I sent my first one out to my list in 1998 (they are called friends-and-family offerings) and oversubscribed it in 2 weeks, raising $1 million.

I've done 4 since, all oversubscribed. Many have asked me how to do it, but they don't have a list; they haven't kept it through the years. My magic list also makes party invitations and Christmas cards a breeze.

## TOOLS FOR SUCCESS –
## USE EMAIL AND TEXTS WHEN EFFICIENT

Emails are by far and away the quickest way to save minutes every day. Texts are even faster. I know, I know. You think that texts are only for the *young un's*. But it is what it is, even my dentist has a service that texts me to remind me of my appointment. Texting is a tool every business owner should use when it is just as effective and saves time.

This series of articles is written by an overachiever that understands he can't do it all by himself, he needs others helping, and there simply aren't enough hours in the day. First, you've got to come to that realization. Then, you can move to seeking ways to do more.

Admittedly, I likely go too far towards using e-mails and texts, as there is very little that can't be done that way. Frankly, I think many folks just aren't that comfortable with change, and they haven't realized that even the small amount of time they save can be put to use doing something else that will make them more successful. Several of the other articles in this series address topics like how to properly delegate and how to squeeze an extra hour out of every day. Make use of the tools that save time, such as texting.

Is it less personal? Does that matter? Of course, but the question is how much does it matter, and is it all the time? Most matters are administrative. Not to mention that you can steal a minute *when you want to,* on your timetable, rather than waiting for others; there is no substitute for a sense of urgency. You can steal time when *only* your phone is available to give an instruction clarification, or answer a question so someone isn't waiting for you. The cumulative effect of that is you speed tasks along to completion.

Another tip is that you must have a good email client, like Outlook. You *young un's* that think you can keep and do everything on your phone are just wrong. You need a good email client so that you can search emails, file and save the important ones, and, most critically, save all documents in document folders, not in the emails. The file structure for your email storage and document storage should be as close to the same as possible. So if you have a folder for *legal* for emails, you should have a document folder named *legal* as well.

Also, critical to success with email, you must handle them, then move them on to a folder or delete them. This makes you very efficient. If it's in your inbox, it's not handled. If you've got more than 20 or so emails in your inbox, you simply aren't very efficient. Try cleaning out your inbox and making it a place where only pending items are kept. Less searching, less stress. Try it.

Also, make sure you always include an email address when you add a contact. I am always amazed the folks that only have a phone number, so of course they take 3 minutes to do something that could have been done, literally, in 10 seconds.

And make sure you have a full contact record for yourself in your phone, and know how to "share" it with others, instead of reading folks your phone number or email address to type into their phone.

Once you really start using emails and text more, others will soon learn that's the best way to reach you and that will give momentum to your new efficiency tool. One other thing, make sure you receive email on your phone as well as your desktop.

## TOOLS FOR SUCCESS — MASTER BLOCKING AND TACKLING

Stop looking for the *Holy Grail*. It doesn't exist. And stop worrying about what your competitor is doing because it appears they are doing better than you. There are *no* secrets and *no* magic formulas. In most cases, you know what to do, but you *aren't* doing it, so you're looking for something that is new and better.

I know, your competitor has a Twitter account so you think you should start to do that and spend more on Facebook. But you haven't even looked at your pitiful web page in 3 years since your cousin's nephew put it up for you.

You're looking to expand your product line, but you've spent no time studying what sells and what doesn't in your current product lines. You aren't tracking any metrics, so all your actions are based on your *gut* instead of any *real data* or industry benchmarks.

Before you are seduced by what is new, work on your blocking and tackling.

Work on the stuff you know works. Devote time to the fundamentals that you've been ignoring. You haven't even bothered to measure anything in years. You haven't reviewed your marketing, your production, your buying, or really much of anything. One thing is for sure, what you used to do *isn't* good enough today. And you haven't spent any time making sure it's all happening like your expected. You haven't looked for ways to improve any of the basics. When you start looking closely, you will be *amazed* by what you find.

Want to cut expenses? Get *serious* about reviewing every financial decision. My boss at Ford, Dixon Thayer, gave us an idea. Look at every expense in the context of, if not done, would we go out of business? If the answer is *no*, then *don't* do it. It's easy to add it back later.

Every business I've ever consulted for had too many employees. Most had been doing the same marketing stuff for years, with little or no thought about how their customers or products might have changed. Read my article about client and prospect acquisition cost and use it to think about your marketing.

I am all about innovation, but the incremental effects of innovation are unlikely to make up for a poor execution of the basics. Never try to grow with a bad foundation; it's a failed strategy. If you can't do the blocking and tackling, you will struggle with innovation, and growth in double-digit percentages is hard to achieve if you aren't on your game.

Too often, I see businesses trying to borrow money to cover operating losses while they try to grow, but that's a terrible mistake unless the owners are on the way to solving the fundamental underlying reasons for a lack of profitability.

## TOOLS FOR SUCCESS – NEVER FORGET THE CUSTOMER IS QUEEN!

Never forget the value of a customer. Certainly, a time comes in every business when you NEED to fire a customer. Here are some reasons I have had for doing so: they would not pay me; they were threatening an employee; they were unprofessional.

Whenever you have to fire a customer, you always want to consider how parting company might affect you. Will you ever encounter them again? How will they take being fired? Are they so vindictive that they may try to harm your reputation online or with other clients? When you have to fire a customer, do it after having thought it out carefully.

One of my favorite books about the positive side of keeping customers is Carl Sewell's *Customers for Life*. Every business owner should read it and make sure every sales and service employee they have also reads it.

My girlfriend, Linda, understands that business is about customer relationships. She has been with State Farm Insurance for more than 20 years and has been a State Farm Agent in Fort Worth for six years. Two times a week, a current client comes to her office and tells her that they intend to move their business to another carrier because of price. She is never defensive, always kind, empathetic, and professional.

Linda listens carefully and is often able to keep those customers because she treats them with kindness and courtesy. By listening and empathizing, Linda is often able to get a client to sit down with her to compare the coverages and learn about the differences that produce the savings. Many appreciate that kind of service and decide to stay with Linda.

When she does lose a customer, Linda always asks for the opportunity to quote when they are up for renewal and some come back to her because she demonstrates that her interest in clients goes far beyond a transaction. Rate is just one of many factors considered when people choose to do business with her. It's also about the quality of service they get.

Good service is rarer than it should be. I recently had a disagreement with a service company. The service rep responded to my complaint by telling me that no one else ever complained about their service. The implication was that I was being unreasonable.

Even if I were being unreasonable, what is the upside of responding to a complaint in a way that implies the fault is with the client? They told me that I was 100% wrong (there's always a second side to every story), then even said I was "spoiled". Even if I were, what did they gain by making the point, except my anger?

Then, they told me that I couldn't find anyone with their credentials and quality to do that job at the price I wanted. Ironically, they are a new business in a crowded niche. New or established, never be so pompous or naïve as to think you are the ONLY one who can do the job.

Then they wanted to discuss all that they did right on the job, rather than discussing the mistake or problem. Again, that isn't going to repair the relationship or keep the customer. Imagine your son telling you how he made almost all B's as a defense when you confront him about a D on his report card.

I fired them very graciously. I promptly hired someone else to do the work. My new vendor is doing a better job for less money. Even though I liked the old vendor, they did not value the relationship with me or did not understand the basics of customer service, and acted on emotion when challenged. Worse still, they did not learn anything from losing my business that might improve their service.

I teach the client-service employees at my companies to deal with customers by listening, empathizing, and acting to correct the issue. We spell out the steps we will take to fix the issue and ensure it does not happen again. We apologize and we fix it. We're about solutions that are win-win and strengthen the relationship with the customer.

Don't get caught up in thinking about one transaction. Keep your eye on the lifetime value of the customer whose issue you need to solve. What is all of his or her future business worth? What are the referrals that he or she could send you worth? Think lifetime value, not single transaction, and you will find it gets easier to keep customers for life.

## TOOLS FOR SUCCESS –
## KNOW YOUR CLIENT ACQUISITION COST

This has to be my second favorite topic, but admittedly I am a numbers guy. I am all about metrics, numbers, and financials. This article is about something so simple, yet most business owners don't think about it. Client acquisition cost is exactly what it sounds like, i.e., what does it cost you to get one new client?

You may have an idea what your cost is, or what a good or bad cost is, but it varies from business to business. In my consulting for different types of businesses, I have seen huge acquisition costs and really cheap ones.

As a starting point, you can divide your total advertising expenses by the number of new clients. That's only a starting point, however, as you likely get some new clients from referrals or just by walk ins.

I served on an internet game company's board for a while. Their subscribers paid $15 per month to play the game, and the typical subscriber stayed for 6 months, spending a total of $90. It's easy to see that you can't spend too much getting a customer that will only spend $90.

That doesn't preclude expensive mediums, however. Their cheapest client acquisition cost was from TV commercials. That's a shocker! A carefully chosen TV show that cost $750 to run a commercial on would net them 25 new customers, so they had a client acquisition cost of $25. (The $750.00 divided by the 25 new clients). With an average $90 sale, they had a gross margin of $65, or a 61% gross margin and 39% cost of sales.

Because of what a customer is worth, a new car dealer can spend hundreds to get a new client, and a company selling time-shares in jet usage can spend thousands.

To get an idea of what you can spend, think about what you sell and what your gross margin is, and how many times the client will buy. One thing is for sure, if you spend too much, you won't be able to make a profit.

## PROSPECTS, CLIENTS AND CLOSE RATES

More of that pesky math, sorry. In most cases, you will want to track prospects, as not every prospect buys something. And you will want to track close rates. If your event is measured with actual sales, then prospect and client acquisition costs are synonymous.

Prospect acquisition cost is just what it sounds like. Divide your event cost by the number of leads you have. If you spend $500 to have an event, and get 20 leads, then it cost you $25 per prospect or lead.

Close rate is also just what it sounds like. If you get 20 leads at a cost of $25 per lead, and you close half of them (sell them something), your close rate is 50% your client acquisition cost is $50. (Divide your prospect cost by the close rate percentage).

My experience tells me that in most industries a 25% close rate is likely good, though it can be much higher or lower. You likely know this number, you just never thought about it. Your best salesperson works 250 leads per month, and gets 35 new clients, for a 7% close rate.

Start with that as a benchmark and measure and show everyone everyone's close rate, to encourage improvement against their own number, while trying to improve against their peers as well. You will be surprised how all the boats float higher, as those that focus on close rates close more.

My experience says there is no better way to evaluate sellers than their close rate. When you shine a flashlight on it, it will get attention.

Now back to prospect and client acquisition costs. I am always amazed at the folks that run ads in the local newspaper. Restaurants are a good example. They put in a coupon, and dutifully renew it weekly. When you ask them, they will tell you they don't get many, but they love getting some new customers, and the ad does bring some.

When you use the math to demonstrate to them that they are paying $100 or more to get a new client, with a $25 tab, they get it. FAST.

I am not proposing that you stop advertising, or cold calling, or running specials. I just want you to think about which medium has the lowest client acquisition cost, and use it more. You will lower your expenses while you build revenues.

Generally, the internet is the cheapest way to get new clients, but it has to be properly done, using search engine optimization, which most small businesses don't understand. They put up a web site, don't do anything else, and then complain because it didn't bring them new business. It's a sizable portion of my consulting practice, helping small business owners understand how to use the internet to get clients.

Most web developers don't get it either, so listening to them just adds costs with no benefit. You must find a web designer who understands your business proposition and how to help you achieve your goals on the web.

You can use prospect and client acquisition cost in conjunction with the growth matrix optimizer tool I discuss in another chapter to leverage your efforts. If two events have a similar prospect acquisition cost, but the audience is different, and the close rate significantly different, you get a very different client acquisition cost.

For instance, you likely realize that the farther away from your business the event is, the less likely you can close leads. You may get the same number of leads, but the event in your backyard might have a 25% rate, while the event 25 miles away only has a 5% close rate.

So, with the same expenses and number of leads, one event produces 5 times as many clients, and 80% less client acquisition cost. Similarly, if you try to sell symphony tickets in the poorest part of town, you are going to have a lower close rate than when you sell in the higher income part of town.

Understand your prospect acquisition cost, close rate, and your ultimate client acquisition cost to make the most of your marketing and events budget.

## Tools for Success – You Can't Make It on Your Own!

You are unlikely to achieve maximum success on your own. You need people to *like* you and want to see you do well. When others like you, they can buy into your goal, and you get everyone pulling on the oars at the same time, the same way. Your results will be catapulted to success, because you will use the leverage of others.

When others are bought into your goal, and like you, you can delegate to them, which allows you to work on other initiatives or new ideas. The ability to work on initiatives concurrently allows you to do so much more. My friends used to say that I threw 100 ideas at the wall, and only a few stuck, but they were *humdingers*. Having others helping you will free your mind to be more creative and teach you to be more collaborative.

But it's not just about the leverage of people working for you; you need others to like you. If your banker really likes you, he's more likely to loan you money. It's almost a certainty you won't have enough of your own money to reach your goals; you need leverage. You need your attorney to like you so he takes your call and completes documents for you on a Saturday for a Monday, last-second deadline.

The list goes on and on. You need a reputation for being fair, generous, transparent, and honest, while being direct. People appreciate directness with some diplomacy. My old employees at the company I sold have told me many times they wish I was back there, because they always knew where they stood with me, versus the public company where they don't feel as valued or as well informed. I always chuckle and remind them that they've forgotten how many times I changed commission plans or made new work rules they didn't like.

And one other thing, you will struggle to reach financial success unless you stop being cheap. You should be a bootstrapping entrepreneur and be prudent with your money. But no one likes someone who is cheap. We all have one of those friends who tries to get the last nickel out of every deal. Make sure that you always buy the Girl Scout cookies from the mom who works for you or make a donation to the kid's softball team.

And I have a Ron's rule 101 for those who believe I owe them money. If they say I owe them money, (perhaps I disagree because they didn't do a job as agreed or they are just trying to rip me off by manipulating a misunderstanding), as long as it's not a large sum (say, less than $10,000), I will pay.

My rule is I would rather pay you what you say I owe you, and always be able to say you cheated me, than to ever have you be able to say I cheated you. If it is a dispute over a significant sum, we may have to meet at the courthouse to resolve it. Most disputes, however, are about small amounts of money. I am also quick to point out, as I pay, that we will no longer be doing business, but I have paid you everything you said I owed.

Little things can haunt you, so take care of people, and they will be on your team forever.

## TOOLS FOR SUCCESS —
## HOW MUCH DOES PROCRASTINATION REALLY COST YOU?

It's easy to rationalize putting off something you know you should be doing to build your business. It is particularly easy for entrepreneurs, because we're busy and the day-to-day work of getting and keeping clients often gives us the perfect excuse to ignore projects that have strategic payoffs.

One of my favorite sayings is that you don't know what you don't know. It certainly applies to procrastination. Some years back, I served on the board of an internet-gaming company in which I was an investor. This firm had *big* plans. It intended to grow and to become the dominant player in its segment of historical air warfare games.

The company had a good game and the game's creators understood the technology necessary to make game play seem realistic. The technical people assured the board and investors that the firm's system was robust enough to handle 500,000 players, even though they had only between 2,000 and 5,000 players on any given day at the time.

"Don't worry. It will scale," they said. However, we didn't know what we didn't know.

At the time, Microsoft featured a computer game on their home page every day. One day, they chose our game! That day, 100,000 players arrived to try our game in the space of an hour. Our server went down and stayed down until the following morning, when our usual 2,000 to 5,000 players showed up.

We had our big day to shine and we were not ready because we hadn't prepared for success. The company limped along and eventually failed, but it could have been very different had the team not put off testing whether our systems really would scale.

Recently, I was helping another business owner. I had been trying to get him to focus on updating his website because online presence is a crucial part of marketing in his industry. He was always "working on it," but he never seemed to reach the goal posts. A year passed and he still had the same dated site up.

One day, this owner received the sort of surprise business owners dream about. He was booked to appear as a guest on national television. The show has a nightly audience composed of millions of customers interested in what he sells. He had a week to do what I had been asking him to do for more than a year and couldn't get it done.

How much did the procrastination cost him? It's hard to know. Certainly, the appearance gave him the opportunity to get as much traffic in a day as he had gotten in several years. Not being ready cost him the chance to shine.

How can you ensure you will be ready to take advantage of life's opportunities? The simple answer is to have a sense of urgency in all you do. Had this businessperson broken down the web project into its component steps and set a goal with a deadline for each, he would have had a beautiful site done when opportunity arrived.

A goal without a deadline is a dream. It's fine to dream, but take the goal-setting steps and practice urgency so that you can make the most of your share of golden opportunities. When you are working on goals, you can always make course corrections. If you miss, so what. Adjust the deadline and keep right on driving for the goals that matter.

Much of the success that I have had in business and life comes from knowing that I don't have to do it perfectly. You don't either. You only need to do enough to win and very often focusing 50% effort in the right areas is enough to get you 80% or better of the way to victory. Sometimes, details matter, but other times they only slow you down.

A plan that is 80% right and gets implemented and adjusted based on real-world results is much better than a plan that never gets off the ground because the person trying to make it happen insists on having the perfect plan before taking action. Don't let your desire for perfection stop you from starting. After all, you can't win unless you play.

Think about the strategic initiatives that are in your "I'll finish it someday" pile. How many of them could you get to an 80% level if you broke them down, set deadlines, and accepted some imperfection along the way?

Whatever the project or initiative you're dreaming of, set some deadlines and get it going. Set a date NOW. Cycle back and check on it, fine-tuning, if necessary. LATER.

# CHAPTER 11

# LINDA ALLEN:
# GOAL SETTING FOR SUCCESS

*"A goal without a deadline is a dream."*

—Linda Allen

Fort Worth State Farm Insurance Agency Owner Linda Allen

In a recent *Monday Morning Memo*, Small-Business Advertising Consultant and Genius Copywriter Roy Williams wrote, "You meet only four people on the ocean of Life, but you meet them again and again."

The *drifter* is controlled by her or his circumstances. The *drowner* begs for sympathy and hopes for a rescuer. The *surfer* seeks the buzz that comes from being in early on the latest trend.

Finally, the *navigator* charts her or his own course. *Navigators* check the wind, read the charts, and set sail for the destination they have chosen.

I think Roy Williams' types are spot on. Those who become the most successful as entrepreneurs in the beauty business do so because they are *navigators*. They know how to set and achieve powerful goals.

I would like to share five tips that I used to set and achieve professional and personal goals:

- **Write your goals down** – The probability of achieving a goal increases the moment you write it down because a written goal can be scrutinized. A written goal can be tested to see whether it is specific and measurable.

- **Set a deadline** – The gym where I work out has a bulletin board by its door. Trainers encourage members to tack motivational messages to it. On a yellow sticky note, one member posted this: "I want to break records like Mike." Another wrote, "I want to bench press my body weight by September 1." My money is on him because he knows how to write a goal. As my favorite recycler, Ron Sturgeon, is fond of saying, "A goal without a deadline is a dream."

- **Do a weekly review** – Success Coach Jim Fannin, author of *SCORE for Life* and motivational coach to many of the world's top athletes, suggests building time in to do a quick review of your goals every week. He calls it "going to higher ground" because the high ground gives us the best view of where we are on the journey.

- **Be bold** – President Kennedy promised that an American would walk on the moon before the end of the 1960s. On July 20, 1969, *Eagle* touched down. Do you have a goal bold enough that you will forever remember the moment you achieve it?

- **Set a giving goal** – Enrich your life by setting a giving goal (or adding to those you have). Become a mentor to someone who wants a career in the beauty business. Join a service club or use your talents in another way that fits your values and desired legacy.

The goal-setting talent of the *navigators* is part of their secret to creating the lives they envision, having more fun, and getting more done. Set your goals. Chart your course. Enjoy your journey. If one of your goals is to be a better marketer, I recommend subscribing to Roy's free weekly *Monday Morning Memo* newsletter.

# Chapter 12

# Marketing Plan
# and Checklists

The most important challenge every independent beauty professional faces is how to get and keep a steady stream of clients. Marketing a salon requires significant effort. You should read over the ideas in this plan carefully and consider how you can adapt them to your business.

Decide on how fast you want to grow your following and then make a plan to spread the world about your business to enough people consistently to bring you that number of new clients. Whichever elements you choose from this plan, write out your individual marketing plan for your salon. Include estimates of the time that it will take for each activity and the results you expect.

Hold yourself accountable for carrying out the plan every day and every week. Measure results. Did you get the number of new clients you expected? If not, consider whether to expand your existing marketing activities or add new ones to get you to the desired level of appointments.

Keep score so that you know how much time on average each marketing effort takes to produce a new customer. This will help you see how much time you have to invest in marketing to get your book to the level you want it.

In the early stages of your business, expect to spend more time marketing. Even if you have a following, you will still want to market aggressively when you become an independent.

To get you started, daily, weekly, and monthly checklists follow the marketing plan. You should use these as a model to create your own lists based on the marketing activities you have chosen from the marketing plan template.

Every day you should have several marketing activities to do. If your book is not as full as you want it to be, the answer is to devote that time to creatively marketing your business.

1. **Business cards** - Always have business cards, brochures, and flyers available. Include your salon's name, address, phone number, operating hours, website URL and any social media accounts. Stay well stocked and pass them out EVERY DAY. Be proactive in talking to people about your new salon. Vistaprint is an excellent source for attractive business cards.

   **Tip**: Make your card worth something (10% off any service, $5 off, etc.) to encourage people to come see you sooner rather than later.

2. **Website** - Buy a domain name and create a website. This should feature your complete line of services

offered with prices, information about your business, your contact info, and any specials you run.

**Tip:** Some sites where you can get free or inexpensive domains are www.salonbuilder.com; Vistaprint.com; GoDaddy.com; and Web.com. Services like Wix offer easy tools to help you build an attractive website for your salon.

3. **Blogs** - Having a blog with great content can boost your credibility and help potential customers find your business. Regularly add content to your blog that shows potential customers the quality of your work and helps them to see you as an expert in your field. Adding original and fresh content regularly will improve your rankings in search engines like Google and keep the people who read your blog interested and up to date on your business.

**Tip:** Go to www.blogger.com, www.wordpress.com, www.tumblr.com.

4. **Facebook** - Free networking every day! Facebook also offers pay-per-click advertising that will display next to the profiles of those who fit your target market. Since you will only pay if an interested party actually clicks on your ad and goes to your website, these ads can be inexpensive.

**Tip**: Two new useful Facebook features are ideal for salon marketing. First is the ability to 'highlight' posts. In simple terms, a highlighted post makes the particular post twice the size of a standard one. To 'highlight' a post, simply click on the star icon at the top right-hand corner of the post. You can also 'pin' a post. This forces it to the top of your salon timeline, where it will stay for 7 days and then return to chronological order. Make any pinned posts visually attractive and attention grabbing.

5. **Twitter** - Tweet and retweet industry relevant content and balance informational posts with promotional ones. You can even feature online contests to get followers and subscribers more involved. Regularly link tweets back to your website to encourage your followers to visit. If you've got a special offer, then mention it in your tweet and put a link to the offer page.

   **Tip:** Don't have a Twitter account? Go to www. twitter.com to set up your free profile. It's easy. Follow artists you admire for creative inspiration!

6. **Create a portfolio** – Always take before and after shots of your clients, especially when you expect the differences to be dramatic. With permission from your client, add the shots to your portfolio so you can show potential clients looks you have created. Also, with permission, share the photos on your social media and salon site. Be sure to give posts titles that are descriptive. For example, pixie cut and color, etc.

   **Tip:** Have both a physical portfolio and an online portfolio. Some clients want to see your book and others will want to see your work online. Be ready to serve either kind of client.

7. **Instagram & Pinterest** – That portfolio of pictures you just made? Post them online! Two great free social media sites that allow you to easily share

photos and connect with others are Instagram and Pinterest. Most clients won't mind if you post their photos, but always ask permission first. Photos can be a great way to spread the word about your styling ability.

8. **Local businesses** - Talk to other local businesses around you. See if you can put a stack of flyers in their lobbies or ask if they would mind putting your flyers in their customers' bags when they check out. They will most likely want you to reciprocate, so be sure to offer to put their flyers in your space.

9. **Google, Yelp, Yellow pages** - Register your business for free with each of these websites. These sites are essentially online directories. The more places you can be found online, the better. Submit your basic business information, add a link to your website, and encourage your customers to go to these sites and give a review of their salon experience with you.

   **Tip**: Offer incentives or discounts for clients who give you reviews. Their stellar review can turn into more clients in your chair, so encouraging reviews is worth it. Some review sites, such as Yelp, forbid offering incentives for reviews, so be sure you understand how each site works.

10. **StyleSeat** - This is a new and free social networking site for salon professionals! StyleSeat allows you to connect with other professionals in the industry, allows customers searching for services in your area to easily find you, and offers an online booking calendar and data reports!

**Tip**: Go to www.styleseat.com to create your free beauty professional profile and check out the cool features this site offers.

11. **Referral incentives** - Encourage word-of-mouth promotion. When you have a happy client in your salon, give her a coupon for a discount if she returns with a friend. Providing incentive for existing clients to promote your services is one way to expand your client base at little cost to you.

12. **Craigslist** - Posting an ad on Craigslist is free! Do it regularly, if not DAILY. Go to www.craigslist.com, choose your state and city, then click "Services", choose the subcategory of "beauty", "creative" or "therapeutic", and write a simple post about a product or service you would like to feature that day, and include your contact information and appropriate images.

    **Tip**: Try posting in each of the above categories to maximize your reach. Also, post in the "For Sale" category, under the "beauty+hlth" sub category. Change up the services or products you are promoting in the ads to keep the ads from becoming too repetitive. Measure which ads bring you customers and then refine your efforts.

13. **Place ads in local programs & magazines** - Put ads in local coupon books and magazines. Many of these are inexpensive, although it depends on the quality of the book. Offer to barter with the owners in exchange for ad space.

    **Tip:** Make sure you consider your costs carefully. Be sure your ad includes your unique selling propositions and testimonials from your happy clients!

14. **Online booking** – This is a trend in the beauty business. Online booking is extremely convenient for many clients. Several free websites can help you to offer this feature to your customers.

    **Tip:** StyleSeat and BookedIn are two tools that allow you to add online booking. Ask other stylists which online booking tools they use. Try out a tool before committing to a yearly agreement.

15. **Groupon & Living Social** - The online coupon market is a way to gain many new customers. Go to www.groupon.com or www.livingsocial.com to get started. Think of services you can combine to create a discounted package deal for new clients.

    **Tip:** Make sure your website is up and running before negotiating your deal with Groupon or Living Social. They need to know you are a legitimate business.

16. **Send press releases to local newspapers & magazines** – Press releases are a mainstay of basic PR. Don't let it intimidate you – it's simply about sharing news about your business. News outlets are always interested in stories about new trends and styles or new hires. A story on a popular local news site can help people find you.

    **Tip**: The top four FREE press release websites are 24-7 press release, prurgent.com, itdirector.com, prlog.com, and pressbox.com. Need help writing a press release? Google how to write a press release to get tips.

17. **Network/pass out your promo material to niche businesses owners** – Network with local art gallery owners, Sushi restaurant owners, Pilates/spinning/yoga/aerobics instructors, and dance studio owners, etc. Marketing to specialized businesses like these allows you to connect with businesses that likely serve many people who are good prospects for your services. If you earn just a handful of "prime" clients, this tactic can deliver MANY word of mouth referrals.

18. **Direct mail** – Send a postcard to all households within a 1-mile radius or pick the closest zip code. Ask them about postal discounts mailing. Make sure to include an introductory offer for new clients and to make the phone number and other contact information easy to find on the card.

    **Tip:** Many free websites can help you with your direct-mail campaign. **Google free direct-mail marketing.**

19. **Get your salon on Google Maps** – Simply create a Google or Gmail account, log in, and then click on "Business Solutions." Click on "Local Business Center" and create your Google Maps business entry. This service is free and is a great way to make sure Google users find you.

20. **Radio ads** - Make inquiries to radio stations about their advertising solutions. Some stations will give you advertising with no out-of-pocket expense if you donate a certain number of gift certificates to be sold for half price on the station's website. In

return, you get a live interview on the radio, website exposure, and mentions of your salon on the air.

21. **Advertise in local newspapers** - If you want to focus on the neighborhood around your salon, an ad in a community paper can be a low-cost way to reach thousands of local people. Be sure your advertisement also runs in the digital version of the newspaper and on social media pages for the newspaper.

    **Tip**: Choose a paper that is offered free in the area to increase the chances of your ad being seen.

22. **Team-up with local photographers & models** - A hair stylist is essential for photographers that consistently team up with models. After all, a model's hair must look good before and during her photo-shoot. If you are able to partner with a well-known photographer, you can be their go-to stylist. Not only will this enable you to promote your salon to a number of qualified clients, but you will also get credit as the stylist when the photos get published.

    **Tip:** A great place to find local photographers and models is modelmayhem.com. Create a free profile and network away!

23. **Participate in public events** – When there are art festivals or city activities, set up a booth. You can demo a free service, distribute discount coupons, and promote your business.

    **Tip:** Go to your city's webpage to keep an eye on the community calendar for opportunities to promote yourself.

24. **Credit card processing** – Taking credit card payments is a way that you can cater to more clients. Not everyone carries cash or uses checks. NOT having the ability to process credit or debit payments can cost you potential clients.

    **Tip:** Square offers free equipment for processing that works with your smart phone! Go to squareup.com/register to get your free Square!

25. **Have a business email and use it** – Set your email account up so that emails come to your phone. Return emails from prospects and clients promptly. Try to answer them within an hour of when you get them. Although some of your prospective clients may not like email, many will. Be responsive and capture this business. Because few stylists respond quickly to email, you will stand out.

    **Tip:** Ask for email addresses from your existing clients and prospects. Compile them and regularly do email campaigns, coupons, promotions, specials, etc. Constantcontact.com is a good place to find the tools to make managing your lists easy!

26. **Create your own YouTube channel** – Post one video per month; it's easy and free! YouTube.com. You can make the videos using your smart phone. They can be anything from talking about your services, demonstrating a technique that you love, a tutorial on various services, or just information on the latest trends.

    **Tip:** Keep them short and interesting, then tag the video with key words to help the videos get found by potential clients. Choose keywords such as *hairstyles, make-up, beauty tips, hair extensions,* etc. Remember to add tags for the city where your salon is located to help with local search.

## DAILY MARKETING PLAN

Do each of these things daily. They will take only a few minutes each and will keep your prospect pipeline fresh and full!

1. Pass out your business cards. (#1)
2. Post (or renew) a free ad on Craigslist. (#12)
3. Be active on Style Seat. (#10)
4. Facebook/Tweet/Instagram (#4, #5, #7)
5. Call one local business per day – give incentive offer to employees. (#8)
6. Do one short blog posting on a social site with contact and service info. Post pictures of your work! Share the images on Instagram or another photo-sharing site and link to your post. (#3)

## WEEKLY MARKETING PLAN

Complete these marketing strategies weekly to keep your web presence fresh so you will regularly stay in front of potential clients!

1. Post a deal of the week on your website (#2)
2. Update your business Facebook/Style Seat profile (#4, #10)

3. Pass out flyers (#1, #8)

4. Network with a new niche local business owner (#17)

5. Post at least one client review/recommendation to each of your profiles. (#7, #10)

6. Add a picture of recent work to your portfolio! (#6)

## MONTHLY MARKETING PLAN

These marketing tasks should be done at least once every month to get enough exposure to keep new clients coming in.

1. Run a monthly email coupon campaign (#25)

2. Participate in a local public event (#23)

3. Update your portfolio (#6)

4. Direct Mail offer to a small local target market (#18)

5. Put an ad in a local magazine/program (#13)

6. Post a YouTube video on your YouTube channel. (Don't forget to tag it with keywords!)

# About the Authors

**RON STURGEON** is a classic American entrepreneur. His rags-to-riches story began when, at the age of 17, he launched his own auto salvage business after his dad died and he had no money and no place to live. He went on to build it into one of the largest operations of its kind in the United States.

In 1999, he sold his chain of salvage yards to Ford Motor Company. He repurchased what had become a money-losing business from Ford several years later. After whipping it back into profitability, Sturgeon and two partners sold it once more to Schnitzer Industries.

Today Sturgeon is a successful real estate investor and founder of Mr. Mission Possible small business consulting. He is also the founder of the DFW Elite Toy Museum.

Sturgeon is the author of a slew of popular business books including *Peer Benchmarking Groups, Green Weenies, How to Salvage Millions from Your Small Business, How to Salvage More Millions from Your Small Business,* and *Getting to Yes with Your Banker.*

David Blackstock
(Photo credit: Alan Mercer)

**DAVID BLACKSTOCK,** founder of the award-winning Salon Six 9, is proud to introduce his newest salon: Blackstock Studio. Located at Phenix Salon Suites in Fort Worth, TX, Blackstock Studio is the premier destination for one-on-one styling consultation and services.

As Fort Worth's most talented and multifaceted stylist and consultant, David celebrates his third decade in the celebrity-style genre. In addition to his local and regional clientele, David is also personal stylist to Hollywood legends Ruta Lee and Mamie Van Doren, as well as best friend and *confidant* to ever-glamorous and alluring Gennifer Flowers.

David has had a career deeply rooted in the entertainment industry, having worked on numerous regional and national theatre productions, as well as on Broadway productions.

David's styling has been seen on television programming such as *Talk of The Town* (Los Angeles), CNN's *Larry King Live*, NBC's *Today Show*, ABC's *Politically Incorrect*, CBS's *CSI: Crime Scene Investigators*, celebrity news media *The Insider*, the *Biography Channel*, and Showtime's *La La Land*.

# GREAT BOOKS
# MAKE FANTASTIC GIFTS

Order any of Ron's other books by visiting Mr. Mission Possible. com.

*Green Weenies and Due Diligence* is a fun romp through the jargon of the boardroom. Ron compiled this fun dictionary for all those wishing to know the difference between a church revival and a come to Jesus meeting. Illustrated by Gahan Wilson, famed cartoonist for *Playboy*. Available in R-rated and G-rated versions.

*Getting to Yes with Your Banker* is the pocket guide for any entrepreneur wanting to get the most from a banking relationship. Tips for finding the right banker and every part of working with bankers. Written by Ron and Greg Morse, founder and president of Worthington National Bank.

*Peer Benchmarking Groups* – Your guide to using this million-dollar business-building secret from experienced group facilitator Ron Sturgeon.

*How to Salvage Millions from Your Small Business* is Ron's first book designed to share the timeless principles he learned while building his yard into one of the most successful in the USA. Nuts and bolts business building advice from a master!

*How to Salvage More Millions from Your Small Business* is the follow up to Ron's popular guide for entrepreneurs. Get Ron's follow up to his popular guide for business owners.

*409 Low-Cost Events to Promote Your Business* by Ron Sturgeon and Linda Allen. Unlock the potential of events to bring you high-value clients. A complete program for promoting any business with events.

# ORDER FORM

Online Orders: www.MrMissionPossible.com
E-Mail Orders: JenniferK@RDSInvestments.com
Fax Orders: (469) 342-8230
Phone Orders: (817) 834-3625, ext. 232
By Mail: 5940 Eden, Fort Worth Texas 76117

**Products:**

| Title | Price | Quantity | Subtotal |
| --- | --- | --- | --- |

The Insider's Guide to Earning $100k
as an Independent Salon Pro $19.95

Sales Tax* _____
Shipping & Handling** _____
TOTAL _____

\* Sales Tax: Please add 8.25% tax for products shipped to Texas addresses.
\** Shipping and Handling: (US) Add $4 for first book and $2 for each additional book.
Call for international pricing and bulk order discounts.

**Shipping:**
Name: _____
Address: _____
City, State Zip: _____
Telephone: _____
E-Mail Address: _____

**Payment:**
☐ Check enclosed    ☐ VISA    ☐ MasterCard
Card Number: _____
Exp. Date: _____
Security Code: _____
Signature: _____
Name on card: _____
Billing Address: _____
City, State Zip: _____